Emerging Issues in Family Support

Monographs of the American Association on Mental Retardation, 18

Michael J. Begab, Series Editor

Emerging Issues in Family Support

Edited by
Valerie J. Bradley
James Knoll
John M. Agosta

Copyright © 1992 by the American Association on Mental Retardation, formerly the American Association on Mental Deficiency

Published by
American Association on Mental Retardation
1719 Kalorama Road, NW
Washington, DC 20009

The points of view herein are those of the authors and do not necessarily represent the official policy or opinion of the American Association on Mental Retardation. Publication does not imply endorsement by the Editor, the Association, or its individual members.

No. 18, Monographs of the America Association on Mental Retardation (ISSN 0895-8009)

Library of Congress Cataloging-in-Publication Data

Bradley, Valerie J.
　Emerging issues in family support / edited by Valerie J. Bradley, James Knoll, John M. Agosta.
　　p.　　cm.—(Monographs of the American Association on Mental Retardation, ISSN 0895-8009: 18)
　Includes bibliographical references.
　ISBN 0-940898-29-2: $24.95
　1. Handicapped children–Home care—United States.　2. Chronically ill children—Home care—United States.　3. Handicapped children—Respite care—United States. 4. Chronically ill children—Respite care—United States.　I. Knoll, James.　II. Agosta, John M., 1951-　　III. Title.　IV. Series.
HV888.5.B72　　1992
362.1'4'083—dc20　　　　　　　　　　　　　　　　　　　　　　　92-26274
　　　　　　　　　　　　　　　　　　　　　　　　　　　　　　　　　　　CIP

Printed in the United States of America

Table of Contents

Foreword, Fran Smith	vii
Chapter 1 **Overview of the Family Support Movement,** Valerie J. Bradley	1
Chapter 2 **Being a Family: The Experience of Raising a Child with a Disability or Chronic Illness,** James Knoll	9
Chapter 3 **Supporting Families: State Family Support Efforts,** James Knoll, Susan Covert, Ruth Osuch, Susan O'Connor, John Agosta and Bruce Blaney	57
Chapter 4 **Evaluating Family Support Services: Two Quantitative Case Studies,** John Agosta	99
Chapter 5 **Family Empowerment: Four Case Studies,** Marsha Langer Ellison, Hank Bersani, Jr., Bruce Blaney and Elissa Freud	151
Chapter 6 **Conclusions and Implications,** Valerie J. Bradley	167
About HSRI and the Editors	175

Foreword

By 1958, at age 24, I had four children under four, two of whom had cerebral palsy. For the next several years I struggled to stay ahead of the unending tasks each day held: lifting, carrying, bathing, feeding, folding diapers, dressing, toileting, folding clothes and diapers, cooking, cleaning, positioning, structuring play, folding diapers, all the while caring for the "special needs" of two youngsters who needed regular therapies and periodic surgeries and trying to be a super mother and wife. And then one day the marriage was over. I found myself a single mother doing all of the above (except folding diapers) *and* working an eight-hour job each day *and* attempting to schedule special events into our lives to make up for the absence of a father; sometimes working an additional job on weekends to pay for the babysitters.

Our life was dictated by what we could do, where we could go, with two wheelchairs. Throughout these years many well-meaning professionals had advised me to "place" my oldest daughter, where she would be happier "with her own kind." After another three years of this schedule, I finally did "place" my daughter. I was heartbroken. I was outraged. I had failed. She would suffer.

It would be another 11 years before I heard the term *respite*: temporary relief from the continual stresses of raising a child with a disability. The instant I heard the term I knew the magnitude of the changes respite could have made in my family and in all the other families faced with similar circumstances who held on as long as they could but then made a similar choice.

Now I am a professional in the "disability field," working to bring information to parents so that they can enjoy the child they have and build on the strengths of their unique family. Now we know about respite. And even better, we know about family support. We no longer have to struggle with what to do for families with a member who has a disability. The mistakes of the past do not have to be repeated hundreds of times with thousands of families. The lessons that have been learned in the last two decades in states that have forged ahead to support families have been gathered into this document to serve as a beacon to families and a textbook to professionals, policy makers, and would-be change agents.

I am very pleased to write the introduction to this monograph. Both as someone who has felt the injustices of a system that allowed our family to be severed and as a professional striving to create change in numerous states, I recognize the value of each chapter. I also know of the dedication and integrity of each of the principal writers. Valerie Bradley, Jim Knoll, and John Agosta have talked with, met with, and worked with thousands of families in the last 10 years. They are not only aware of research findings and best writings on the topic of family support, they are, in fact, leading researchers and authors. They have carried these messages to professionals and policy makers in numerous states.

It is true that children with disabilities do best "with their own kind." But their own kind are their families, friends, neighbors, and schoolmates. Family support, when in place, allows children to thrive in such an environment and families to become more competent. Dear reader, please, use this monograph to build on what we have in place until we create a seamless system of supports for all families in every state in the nation.

Fran Smith

Chapter 1

Overview of the Family Support Movement

Valerie J. Bradley

BACKGROUND

Frustrated by the lack of opportunities and services, parents have historically initiated programs for their sons and daughters with mental retardation and other disabilities. Most recently, parents have been concentrating their advocacy efforts on the creation of family support programs defined by individual family needs. When conceptualized in this family-centered fashion, family support offers flexible service, focuses on the entire family, changes as family needs change, encourages families to use natural community supports, and provides convenient access to coordinated services and resources.

The first and primary natural environment for members of any society is the family. To say that children belong in families and that their family connections are of lifelong and primary importance states the obvious. However, only in recent years have we begun to recognize that persons with mental retardation and other disabilities are also entitled to be part of a family (Taylor, Knoll, Lehr, & Walker, 1989). This recognition represents a clear break with the past, when families were strongly encouraged by medical and social service professionals to seek institutional placements for children born with severe disabilities (McKaig, 1986).

During the childhood years, over 90% of persons with mental retardation and other developmental disabilities live with their families (Agosta & Bradley, 1985). However, changes in the American family—increased numbers of working mothers, more single parent families, smaller family size, and lack of available extended family—suggest that contemporary families have diminished resources at their disposal to provide the care required by their family member with a disability (Agosta & Bradley, 1985; Schorr, 1988). These demographic changes, coupled with the fact that children with severe, multiple disabilities and complicated medical conditions are surviving past infancy and living at home, point to the need for more and better support of families.

An increasing number of states, with guidance and pressure from parents, have begun to recognize their responsibilities to families and are increasing the support and services they provide (Knoll, Covert, O'Connor, Agosta, & Blaney, 1990). In 1972, Pennsylvania became the first state to initiate a family support project. At this writing, all but a handful of states provide some form of support to families who have children with mental retardation or other disabilities. While respite care is by far the most prevalent support that states provide, an increasing number of states offer a range of services including home and vehicle modification, training, case management, counseling, nursing, and home health care.

It is to the credit of grass roots lobbying efforts by families that the concept of family support is beginning to be accepted at both state and national levels (Smith, Card, & McKaig, 1987). Parents who have advocated before Congress, their state legislatures, and the boards of regional and local service agencies have been successful in initiating or expanding the support and services available to families caring for children with mental retardation or other disabilities.

Parents base their call for family support on the fact that it is the most cost effective service the state can provide. By supporting families and aiding the integration of children with disabilities in their home communities and neighborhood schools, the state will shape the future demand for adult services in a manner that places much greater reliance on the resources that already exist in our communities rather than on more expensive specialized settings. Parents further argue that families should increasingly be included in the design, implementation, and monitoring of family support programs.

In a study completed in 1990, the Human Services Research Institute determined that family support services made up only about 1.5% of the total budget of services for people with developmental disabilities (Knoll et al., 1990). Further, though about 46 states offered some form of family support, it was by and large limited to respite services, and in each of 15 states, less than 100 families were being served. Though each new fiscal year brings substantial growth in family support programs around the country, there are also reports that some programs no longer exist because they were pilot projects that did not become permanent (e.g., in Arkansas). Further, many family support initiatives have not been firmly established by legislative mandate and therefore are susceptible to the vicissitudes of the state budgetary process. These factors underscore the often tentative and embryonic nature of family support efforts in the United States.

The national study also found wide variation in the extent of family supports from state to state. At the time of the study reported in chapter 3, only three states, Michigan, Wisconsin, and Minnesota, had relatively comprehensive programs established by state legislation. Since that time,

Illinois, Colorado, and New Hampshire have also adopted fairly broad-based programs. One other, Louisiana, had new legislation, which will bring close to a comprehensive array of supports when it is fully implemented. At the time of the study, an additional 14 states had some supports that were mandated by state legislation.

While support to families may take a variety of forms, the major goals of state family support programs are to deter unnecessary out-of-home placements, return persons living in institutions back to families, and enhance the care giving capacity of families (Agosta & Bradley, 1985). For example, the Wisconsin Department of Health and Social Services (1985) gives the following explanation of its Family Support Program:

> The program is intended to ensure that ordinary families faced with the extraordinary circumstances that come with having a child with severe disabilities will get the help they need without having to give up parental responsibility and control. (p. 2)

The increasing prominence of the family support movement can be explained by changed expectations among families, an evolution in values in the disability field, and concurrent shifts in program approaches. The movement has also been fueled by the increasing number of children with very severe disabilities living at home. The presence of such children is in part the result of improved neonatal intervention that has reduced mortality among increasingly smaller and more premature infants as well as the availability of a variety of home-based technologies that in the past would have been seen only in hospitals (e.g., respirators, heart monitors, etc.).

The development of family support policy has gone through three distinct phases. In the first period, the era of institutionalization and segregation (roughly ending in the late 1960s), the governing norms were primarily medical, and the impetus was to separate people who were "sick" and vulnerable. During this period, families who had children with disabilities had only two alternatives—to maintain the child at home 24 hours a day or to place the child in the institution. The initiation of two major federal programs toward the end of this era, Medicaid (1966) and Supplemental Security Income (1974), at least made it possible for income eligible families to secure needed therapies, equipment, and other basic supports for their children.

This period was followed by the era of deinstitutionalization and community development (1970s to the mid 1980s). The rationale for this shift in the locus of care was based on the growing acceptance of the developmental model and its presumption that specialized training and therapeutic services could assist people with mental retardation and other developmental disabilities to grow and learn (Bradley, 1978). For families, this era of "active treatment" led to increased services directed at the child with a disability, though not necessarily at the family as a whole. The Individualized Education Plan, mandated by the Education for All Handicapped Children Act (PL 94-142), became the organizing vehicle for the prescription of developmental services such as speech therapy, physical therapy, and behavioral intervention.

The third and current period, the era of community membership, is marked by an emphasis on functional supports to enhance community integration, quality of life, and individualization (Bradley & Knoll, in press). The concept of functional supports offers an alternative to a continuum of specialized services by focusing on the creation of a network of formal and informal supports that a person with a disability needs to meet day-to-day demands in the home and community (Ferguson & Olson, 1989; Taylor, 1988; Taylor, Racino, Knoll, & Lutfiyya, 1987). With respect to children and families, functional supports are viewed as interventions for the family as a whole as well as for the child. The assumption is that the presence of a child with a disability affects the functioning of the family as a whole and that failure to nurture normal family functioning places the child at risk of out-of-home placement (Kobe, Rojahn, & Schroeder, 1991).

This shifting focus away from deinstitutionalization and the establishment of "community-based programs" to community membership and meeting the support needs of individuals in their homes presents new challenges to the service planner and policy maker. One part of the challenge is how to provide support to children and adults with disabilities in their families. Just as moving people out of their home communities to specialized facilities severs important ties with natural supports, removing people with disabilities from their families—especially when they are children—ignores family commitment, disrupts family connections, and deprives the child of the experience of growing and developing in a family unit (Knoll et al., 1990).

RECENT POLICY DEVELOPMENTS

To enhance the practice of family support and to promote sharing of information across states, the Administration on Developmental Disabilities sponsored a conference in Washington, DC, October 30–31, 1990, that brought together parent representatives and staff of Developmental Disabilities Planning Councils in 12 states. At the conclusion of the two-day meeting, the group affirmed the following principles (Administration on Developmental Disabilities, 1990):

> Children, regardless of the severity of their disability, need families and enduring relationships with adults in a nurturing home environment. As with all children, children with developmental disabilities need families

and family relationships to develop to their fullest potential. Adults with developmental disabilities should be afforded the opportunity to make decisions for themselves and to live in typical homes and communities where they can exercise their full rights and responsibilities as citizens.

Family support should be readily available and should not require the family to fight for it.

Families should be involved in planning, designing, and evaluating family support at all levels of the system including federal, state, and local.

Family support services should be community-centered, family centered, integrated, and coordinated.

Family support should be designed to be sensitive to cultural, economic, social, and spiritual differences.

Family support should include interagency coordination and collaboration.

Family support should be directed at the whole family and should be aimed at keeping families together.

Family supports should be flexible. (pp. 7–8)

This direct and committed call to affirm the family, all families, is, despite its apparent simplicity, at the heart of a national re-examination of how human services should be designed and provided. The impetus for developing a family policy is not limited to the field of mental retardation and developmental disabilities, but is being echoed across the human services community. The new report by the National Commission on Children (1991) provides a generic and comprehensive analysis of the needs of families nationwide and advances several family support principles. Some of those that are most pertinent are as follows:

Every American child should have the opportunity to develop to his or her full potential;

Parents bear primary responsibility for meeting their children's physical, emotional, and intellectual needs and for providing moral guidance and direction. It is in society's best interests to support parents in their child-rearing roles, to enable them to fulfill their obligations, and to hold them responsible for the care and support of their children;

Children do best when they have the personal involvement and material support of a father and a mother and when both parents fulfill their responsibility to be loving providers;

The family is and should remain society's primary institution for bringing children into the world and for supporting their growth and development throughout childhood.

Preventing problems before they become crises is the most effective and cost-effective way to address the needs of troubled families and vulnerable children.

Effectively addressing the needs of America's children and families will require a significant commitment of time, leadership, and financial resources by individuals, the private sector, and government at all levels. (pp. xix–xx)

The National Conference on State Legislatures (Wright & King, 1991) has also highlighted the importance of family support policy in a recent monograph on developmental disabilities:

Assistance with at-home care enhances a family's capacity to provide care and improves the quality of life for the entire family, including the member with a disability.

Responsive family support programs provide a wide array of support services for families, whether they are biological, foster, or adoptive. Families' needs vary, and each family should be encouraged to select those services that are most appropriate to build upon its strengths and to meet its needs.

Support services should be available to families from the onset of the disability and should be designed to reach out to families.

Access to family support services should be timely and convenient for families.

As the person with a disability reaches adulthood, the focus on support programs should shift to choices for the individual, whether he or she lives with the family or in another community setting.

The public sector cannot be counted on to meet all family needs. Support services should build on the framework found in the family, the neighborhood, and the community. Employers and private health insurance carriers also should be called on to provide support.

Families should be allowed to control resources, making the system less "provider driven" and more "consumer driven."

Children with disabilities benefit most from training in natural settings where they can learn independent living and work skills that will enable them to live in the community once they become adults or choose to live away from the family home.

Strengthening the family structure may be less costly to the state than funding expensive alternative residential options for children. (pp. 8-9)

All of these policy initiatives and refinements point to a growing national consensus regarding the relationship of healthy family functioning to the well-being of all children regardless of their disabilities or vulnerabilities.

CONTENT OF THIS MONOGRAPH

Family support programs in most states are still relatively new and, as noted above, relatively small. As a result, little systematic information has been gathered on the outcomes of these emerging policies and programs. The ensuing monograph distills some preliminary research that has been conducted by the Human Services Research Institute on family support programs nationally and in several states. Because of the multifaceted character of family support and the importance of multiple perspectives in evaluating such efforts, several methodologies are reflected including quantitative as well as qualitative techniques.

Following this overview, chapter 2 reviews the results of interviews with almost 100 families of children with disabilities around the country and presents a summary of their responses regarding the challenges that they face and the ways in which these challenges have been addressed by public programs.

Chapter 3 presents information on the status of family support at the state level and reflects the findings of a national interview survey conducted in 1989. Although substantial activity regarding family support has occurred since, these findings provide the reader with a notion of trends, constraints, magnitude, and characteristics of family support around the country.

Chapter 4 presents the findings of two quantitative case studies of family support pilot projects in Illinois and Iowa and includes the results of family surveys in those states. This discussion provides data on the impact of flexible funding as well as family support coordinators on the families served. Chapter 5 discusses the findings of a series of qualitative case studies of demonstration family support programs in Pennsylvania. The findings provide information on family satisfaction, the design of local family support programs, and issues surrounding the auspices under which family support programs operate.

The final chapter summarizes policy implications raised by the research described and suggests future directions for the evaluation of family support efforts.

REFERENCES

Administration on Developmental Disabilities. (1990). *Educating policymakers: A nine state perspective. Proceedings of a conference held October 30–31 in Washington, D.C.* Washington, DC: Mayatech.
Agosta, J., & Bradley, V. (1985). *Family care for persons with developmental disabilities: A growing commitment.* Boston: Human Services Research Institute.
Bradley, V. J. (1978). *Deinstitutionalization of developmentally disabled persons: A conceptual analysis and guide.* Baltimore: Brookes.
Bradley, V. J., & Knoll, J. (in press). Shifting paradigms in services to people with disabilities. In O. C. Karan & S. Greenspan (Eds.), *Rehabilitation services in the community.* Andover Medical Publishers.
Ferguson, P. M., & Olson, D. (Eds.). (1989). *Supported community life: Connecting policy to practice in disability research.* Eugene, OR: University of Oregon, Center on Human Development, Specialized Training Program.
Knoll, J. (1989). *Come together: The experience of families of children with severe disabilities or chronic illness.* Available from Human Services Research Institute, Cambridge, MA.
Knoll, J., Covert, S., O'Connor, S., Agosta, J., & Blaney, B. (1990). *Family support services in the United States: An end of decade status report.* Cambridge, MA: Human Services Research Institute.
Kobe, F. H., Rojahn, J., & Schroeder, S. R. (1991). Predictors of urgency of out-of-home placement needs. *Mental Retardation, 29,* 323–328.
McKaig, K. (1986). *Beyond the threshold: Families caring for their children who have significant developmental disabilities.* New York: Institute for Social Welfare Research, Community Service Society of New York.
National Commission on Children. (1991). *Beyond rhetoric: A new American agenda for children and families.* Washington, DC: Author.
Schorr, L. B. (1988). *Within our reach: Breaking the cycle of disadvantage.* New York: Doubleday.
Smith, M., Card, F., & McKaig, K. (1987). *Caring for the developmentally disabled child at home: The experience of low income families.* New York: Community Service Society of New York.
Taylor, S. J. (1988). Caught in the continuum: A critical analysis of the principle of the least restrictive environment. *Journal of the Association for Persons with Severe Handicaps, 13,* 41–53.
Taylor, S., Knoll, J., Lehr, S., & Walker, P. (1989). Families for all children: Value-based services for children with disabilities and their families. In L. Irvin & G. Singer (Eds.), *Support for caregiving families: Enabling positive adaptation to disability* (pp. 41–53). Baltimore: Brookes.
Taylor, S. J., Racino, J., Knoll, J., & Lutfiyya, Z. (1987). *The nonrestrictive environment: On community integration for people with the most severe disabilities.* Syracuse, NY: Syracuse University, Center on Human Policy, Community Integration Project.
Wisconsin Department of Health and Social Services. (1985). *Family support program guidelines and procedures.* Madison, WI: Author.
Wright, B., & King, M. (1991). *Americans with developmental disabilities: Policy directions for the states.* Denver, CO: National Conference on State Legislatures.

Chapter 2

James Knoll

Being a Family
The Experience of Raising a Child with a Disability or Chronic Illness

INTRODUCTION

As we highlight above and explore in more detail in the next chapter, the last decade has seen family support emerge as a major item on the policy agenda of almost every state and increasing federal emphasis on support for "family-centered, community-based" care (Koop, 1987; Maternal and Child Health, 1988; Nelkin, 1987). Present evidence suggests that family support services developed to date do have a positive effect on participating families. Families receiving services report the following:

- Enhanced commitment to continued care at home rather than seeking an out-of-home alternative (Parrott & Herman, 1987; Rosenau, 1983; Zimmerman, 1984);
- Reduced overall stress levels (Moore, Hamerlynck, Barsh, Spieker, & Jones, 1982);
- Increased time spent away from the demands of caregiving, resulting in an improved capacity to keep up with household routines, pursue hobbies, and seek employment outside the home (Moore et al., 1982; Zimmerman, 1984);
- Improved skills for coping with habilitative needs (Moore et al., 1982; Minnesota Developmental Disabilities Council, 1983);
- An improved overall quality of life (Rosenau, 1983);

Acknowledgment. Preparation of this chapter was supported with funds from the National Institute of Disabilities and Rehabilitation Research, U.S. Department of Health and Human Services, through a cooperative agreement (#G0086C3523-88). All opinions expressed herein are solely those of the author and do not reflect the position or policy of the Department of Health and Human Services.

- Willingness to be taught several of the specialized competencies needed to provide habilitative care (Karnes & Teska, 1980; Snell & Beckman-Brindley, 1984).

In sum, the evidence that has been collected documents the efficacy of family-centered, community-based services. Families indicate that they appreciate such services and are satisfied with their effects, including a reduction in levels of stress (Herman, 1983; Rosenau, 1983; Zimmerman, 1984). Further, families report that they benefit most when they are provided with multiple service options (e.g., respite care, financial assistance, and parent education) and least when they are offered fewer services (e.g., respite care only) (Moore et al., 1982). This suggests that no single service component is sufficient for achieving the goals of family support, but that several may be necessary.

Though the above findings lend credence to the efficacy of family support programs, a basic tension in this emerging pattern of family support policy bears careful consideration. The rationale for the first generation of family support laws and regulation was that family support is cost effective because it precludes expensive out-of-home placement. Based on this cost effectiveness argument many states have provided, under Medicaid waivers and various state programs, relatively comprehensive home-based services to families of people with the most severe disabilities who theoretically would be most at risk for placement. Similar arguments have been used to obtain funding for home care for a relatively small number of technology dependent and other medically complex children under the so-called "model waiver" program. The reality, however, is that (a) the vast majority of families have never sought out-of-home placement (Ashbaugh, Spence, Lubin, Houlihan, & Langer, 1985), and (b) through either stated or unstated policy, an increasing number of states bar out-of-home placement of children by depending largely on services provided through special education—so this argument for family support is only partially persuasive.

Increased delivery of services in the family home has forced a reexamination of professional roles and the parent-professional relationship and has spawned concepts such as parent control, partnership, and family empowerment. The power of these concepts, the experiences of the small group of parents who have received services governed by these concepts, and the rave reviews of parents and professionals who have witnessed the effectiveness of these "new models" in the lives of families and children with disabilities and special health care needs have created a growing number of advocates whose aim is no longer merely to develop cost-effective alternatives to institutionalization. Rather it is to make family-centered, consumer-controlled services the model for future service delivery. The result is a ground swell of efforts to expand family support strategies beyond merely deterring institutional placement to meeting the needs of the great majority of families with a child with some special need, families traditionally unserved or served only by the school system. This increased demand for family support may undercut the cost effectiveness argument because the savings that are realized among those at risk of institutional placement may be lost as programs are expanded to meet the needs of a much larger and somewhat less disabled population. Thus, making a case for the expansion of family support will of necessity rely on the inherent benefits of such supports to the family and the ways in which they increase the family's capacity to care for their family member and ultimately their quality of life.

Although data on the benefits of individual family interventions on family functioning exist, little systematic information on family needs is available to answer the key policy questions raised by current efforts to expand family support. The study reported in this chapter was an initial effort to fill this gap. It was based on the premise of a commonality of need among a diverse array of families who have children with developmental disabilities, emotional disturbance, chronic medical conditions, and highly specialized medical needs. Guided by the belief that parent empowerment and control are essential cornerstones of any family support system, we also assumed that the best way to understand what families need is to ask them directly. In the broadest sense, we wanted to know what family support means to families. To answer this overarching question, we addressed three major areas:

- What are the day-to-day issues in raising a child with a disability or chronic medical condition?
- What is the full array of costs (financial, social, personal, and opportunity) associated with raising a child with a disability or chronic medical condition?
- What types of support does a family need to address these issues and meet these costs?

METHODS

To answer these questions, we adopted a methodology that combined elements of survey research with a semistructured interview. Our major goal was to understand how the families thought about their lives and their interactions with the service system. For this reason, in the interviews we tended to avoid asking questions that limited the range of possible responses. For example, instead of asking families to rate a list of possible community services based on their potential helpfulness, we asked whom they turned to for help and asked them to describe how that person or organization helped them. This approach, which is traditionally defined as an exploratory stage for other research strategies, seemed particularly apropos for answering our central question: What does family support mean to families?

Instrument

A 112-item, 57-page data collection protocol was designed in consultation with representatives of most of the principal disability advocacy organizations involved in the Coalition for Citizen with Disabilities (CCD). The protocol attempted to integrate standard forced-choice questionnaire items, which would allow us to develop a quantitative snapshot of the families in our study group and their experience raising a child with a disability or chronic medical condition, with open-ended items, which allowed families to talk about how they actually thought about the question or to describe their experience related to a particular aspect of home care. The protocol was organized around 13 topic areas: characteristics of the household, characteristics of the child, developmental skills, medical complications, physical limitations, sensory disabilities, challenging behavior, impact of disability on the household, financing health care, informal support systems, formal support services, family employment, and perceived service needs.

Study Group Selection

The project advisory group counseled us to take a rather unorthodox approach to selecting our subjects for this study. They felt, along with project staff, that the major foci should be on the common needs and experiences that cut across traditional categorical labels and on understanding the "family experience." They also urged us to sample the range of family experience nationally by selecting subjects from states that represent the diverse approaches to family support (see chapter 3).

The advisory group worked in concert with the project staff to develop some working definitions to assist us in identifying appropriate study participants. The group felt that the first issue that needed to be articulated was the basic distinction between "traditional" developmental disabilities as defined by the Developmental Disabilities Act and chronic medical conditions that presented families with care issues at least equal to those related to the more traditional group. The advisors recommended that the study group be drawn equally from these two basic groups. To further assist in identifying participants, the panel addressed the basic characteristics that distinguish subgroups within the two larger populations. Within the developmental disabilities group, three subgroups, based on the nature of

TABLE 2.1
Subject Categories by Specific Disabling Conditions

PHYSICAL	DEVELOPMENTAL DISABILITIES COGNITIVE	EMOTIONAL
Cerebral palsy Spina bifida Birth defect Major orthopedic impairment (e.g., absence of limb, osteogenesis imperfecta, etc.)	Mental retardation Autism Traumatic brain injury Severe learning disabilities	Emotional disturbance

DEGENERATIVE	CHRONIC HEALTH CONDITIONS EPISODIC	CONSTANT
AIDS Cystic fibrosis Muscular dystrophy Tuberous sclerosis Neurofibromatosis Heart disease	Leukemia Cancer Hemophilia Seizure disorder Sickle cell anemia Severe asthma	Technology dependent (ventilator, apnea monitor, gastrostomy tube, etc.) Dialysis Diabetes

the disability, were identified: physical, cognitive, and emotional/behavior disabilities. Table 2.1 presents some examples of specific conditions or primary diagnoses that were placed in each of these categories. The advisory panel also identified three basic subgroups under chronic medical conditions. These three groupings reflected two considerations, the progression of the condition and the level of care associated with that progression. Table 2.1 presents examples of specific diagnoses in the three health subgroups: degenerative, episodic, and constant.

The project advisory panel nominated eight states to be the focus of data collection based on geographic distribution and diversity in patterns of service delivery: Arkansas, California, Florida, Michigan, Minnesota, New York, Virginia, and Washington. In the initial study design, an equal number of subjects from each of the six subgroups outlined above were to be identified across these eight states.

Fulfilling this ambitious design proved problematic. The local affiliates of all of the organizations participating on the advisory panel were contacted for assistance in making initial contact with families. Unfortunately, many of these local organizations did not have the capacity to assist us in contacting families, while others felt, even with the participation of their national office, that it was inappropriate for them to act as a conduit for a research study that did not clearly fit with what they saw as their mission. As a result, only one or two organizations in each state were willing to work with project staff to identify families.

TABLE 2.2
Study Group by Disability and State

	AR	CA	FL	MI	MN	NY	VA	WA	TOTALS
Developmental Disabilities									44
Cognitive	5	2	1	2	1	2	2	2	17
Physical	5	1	1	2	1	5	2	1	18
Emotional	1	3	—	2	2	—	—	1	9
Chronic Health Conditions									48
Degenerative	1	1	4	2	2	3	2	3	18
Episodic	—	1	3	1	2	3	2	1	13
Constant	—	2	3	4	—	5	1	2	17
Totals	*12*	*10*	*12*	*13*	*8*	*18*	*9*	*10*	*92*

Because many of the cooperating organizations focused very specifically on a particular population, they did not have access to individuals with some of the conditions outlined in the sampling plan. As a consequence, we decided to modify the sampling plan based on the pool of available subjects in each state. For example, in Arkansas we had no point of access to families of children with specialized health care needs, but in New York we had good access to this group. So an attempt was made to have equal participation from families in each of the six groupings but to forego the effort to maintain an equal distribution within each state. This process was further complicated when a family was identified as belonging to one group because of the organization through which we made contact, but when the interviewer finally met the family he or she realized the primary diagnosis of the child clearly placed them in another group.

The cooperating organizations in each state made phone contact with families that most closely fit the selection criteria outlined on the sampling plan, including equal distribution across the age span and participation by racial and ethnic minority groups. If the family indicated an interest in participating, the agency sent them a letter explaining the study in detail and asking their permission to be interviewed. This process took almost nine months to complete. Table 2.2 outlines the distribution of study group participants in each of the six subgroups across the eight target states.

Data Collection

The protocol was administered to the families by 12 data collectors recommended by local affiliates of the organizations serving on the project advisory panel. The interviewers were brought together for two days of intensive training on how to use the protocol and interact with the families. The interviewers had diverse backgrounds: 5 were parent-case advocates associated with family advocacy organizations, 3 were independent consultants who specialized in working with families on issues such as long term planning, 3 were family case manager-social workers from agencies that were not involved with any of the families in the study group, and 1 was a college professor with extensive experience in qualitative research.

It is axiomatic in qualitative research that the success or failure of a research project hinges on the skill and sensitivity of the individual field worker and not on the integrity of the data instrument (Bogdan & Biklen, 1983). In the final analysis, the success of this project was dependent on the fact that each data collector had extensive personal experience with families of people with disabilities or chronic illness. The empathy and respect with which they approached families made it possible for them to establish, in most cases, an immediate rapport with the family member, which was necessary to gain a thoughtful response to the open-ended questions. The somewhat diminished quality of information obtained in the few interviews in which rapport was not achieved confirms this perception.

During the lengthy process of subject recruitment, most of the data collectors worked in concert with the agencies in their state that had agreed to help us identify study group participants. After the agencies identified appropriate families who had expressed a willingness to participate, the field worker called them, explained the study to them again, and arranged to meet them in their home, at their convenience, to conduct the interview. At the interview, the data collector once again explained the study to the family members present and asked them to sign an informed consent form. In a small number of cases, data collectors also asked permission to tape record the conversation and in all cases were granted that permission. In most instances, however, the interviewers preferred to take notes, as most of them felt that the presence of the recorder would create a barrier to rapport. Each family was paid $30 for participating in the study. The interviews lasted anywhere from 3 to 7 hours and yielded rich descriptive information.

Analysis

The unprocessed data forms and field notes were submitted to the project office where all data analysis was performed. All responses to questionnaire items were coded, and descriptive statistics were generated using SPSS (Statistical Program for the Social Sciences). All interview notes were transcribed into a standard form on a personal computer using Microsoft Word. These qualitative data were subsequently read, in their entirety, at least three times by the project field director, who personally conducted all further analysis.

During these readings, recurring topics and common experiences were identified in an effort to organize the common "themes" that capture the experiences of these families. It is these themes which form the basic organization of this report. It should be noted that the identification of these themes was relatively straightforward, since, for all of their seeming diversity, these families had a remarkably similar core experience. During the first reading, a list of statements or topic sentences that seemed to capture the essence of the families' narrative was generated. This list was then reviewed and compressed based on similarities. At the second reading, the individual family anecdotes were compiled in files based on presence of a common theme. The original transcription was reviewed a final time to assure that individual anecdotes were sorted into the appropriate theme files. All subsequent analyses concentrated on review of the thematic files to identify the essence of the experience described and to identify those individual stories which were the best exemplars for the common experience.

RESULTS

This report is the story of 92 families who represent an intentional sampling of the cultural, ethnic, religious, regional, and economic diversity found in the United States. They live in run-down public housing in New York City where they lock themselves in for their own protection, mobile homes in rural Arkansas, and in prosperous middle class suburbs throughout the country. They range from anonymous single parent families who are barely subsisting on welfare to a nationally known celebrity with a six figure income. And yet, the major themes in the stories they each tell are surprisingly similar. In every case, the diversity of these families has been overshadowed by the fact that being a family has been re-defined by the needs of a child with a disability or a chronic medical condition.

It is true that each family and the situation of each child is unique. Several of these families tell what it means to raise an adolescent with diabetes or hemophilia. Others describe the daily challenges of caring for an infant who is dependent on sophisticated medical technology for every breath. In some cases these tell of learning to deal with the development of a child whose learning is hampered by major intellectual, physical, or behavioral disabilities. And, finally, a few recount what it is to live with a child who has a degenerative condition. Yet the clear message that comes through in extensive conversations with these families is that their experiences comprise a collective as well as an individual reality. The commonalities that transcend their diversity clearly point to issues of social significance that merit the attention of decision makers in health and social policy at the local, state, and national level.

As a group, these families find themselves transported by a series of uncontrollable events into a whole new world. Their lives are changed. They find themselves in alien environments where they are forced to deal with a foreign language in a struggle for the well-being of their child and family. Most find themselves pushed to economic limits which they never thought imaginable. They find their social world redefined. In an effort to do the most natural of things—care for their own child—they find themselves confronting a multitude of public and private gatekeepers, any one of whom seemingly has the ability to thwart their efforts. They find themselves involved in a constant round of begging, cajoling, and appealing to higher authorities, often in an effort to obtain the most modest assistance in getting their child's specialized needs met within the home. Yet, with all this, they do persevere and have succeeded in their efforts. Moreover, they are readily able to speak of the positive impacts as well as negative that the experience of a child with a disability has had on them.

The findings presented here are testimony to the willingness of families to open their homes and their private lives to the interviewers. By telling their own stories, these families have convincingly woven common threads into a pattern of triumph tempered with frustration, isolation, stigma, and despair over obstacles placed in the path to family support. *The testimony of these families should persuade policy makers across the public and private spectrum to examine whether the rhetoric about the centrality of home and family life is supported by the day-to-day practices in their organizations.* Finally, the openness of these families imposes a requirement on the readers to really listen to them and hear what they are saying.

The results of this study are organized around 10 topics: the families and their children; the daily routine; taking care of the child; being a family; family, friends, and neighbors; paying the bills; getting what the child needs; family supports; the daily battles; and the future. The first eight sections have a parallel structure. They begin with descriptive statistics from the questionnaire items related to each topic area. This is followed by relevant interview data. In the interview section, a heavy emphasis is placed on allowing the parents to speak for themselves. Wherever possible, the presentation in these sections relies on direct quotations from the field notes in the form of interviewee comments or observations by the data collector.

In regard to the use of quotations within this report, it is necessary to make two points. First, these quotes have been only slightly modified to assure anonymity to the families and to clarify any problems of comprehension that could result when quotes are taken out of context. (In all cases, names used in this report are pseudonyms.) Second, in selecting a

TABLE 2.3
1987 Taxable Household Income (*N* = 88)

INCOME RANGE ($)	% OF GROUP	*n*
<10,000	22.8	21
10,000–19,999	21.7	20
20,000–29,999	12.0	11
30,000–39,999	22.8	21
40,000–49,999	4.3	4
>50,000	12.0	11

quote, an effort has been made to assure that although the specifics of each situation are unique, the central point stands as an exemplar for the experience of the entire group. We have avoided using quotations that describe a set of circumstances that is entirely idiosyncratic to one family or a very small group of families.

Each quotation is followed by a state abbreviation and a two-digit number in parenthesis. The two-digit number is a randomly assigned identifier to assist in the management of data and to allow the reader to identify quotations which come from the same source.

The last two results sections—the daily battles and the future—are drawn almost entirely from interview data and our synthesis of the information contained in them. Here we continue to use direct quotations from field notes as a major part of our data presentation. In these sections also we have observed the rules outlined above regarding the use of quotes that are generalizable.

Families and Their Children

In 84 of the 92 cases, one of the birth parents of the child with specialized needs was interviewed for this report. The average household in the study group had 4 residents. In 15.6% of the cases, there was only one adult in the household; the balance had two or more adults in the home. In 71.7% (*n* = 66) of the cases the mother was the primary caregiver. The father fulfilled this role in 1 case and grandparents in 3 cases. The balance of the respondents (23.9%, *n* = 22) indicated "other" or left this item blank. A review of the forms indicated that in many of these latter cases, a nurse or other home health care worker was identified.

The average household in the study group had an income in the $20,000–$29,999 per year range. Table 2.3 provides a breakdown of the income distribution of the study group. In 57% of the cases, the person we interviewed worked outside of the home for an average of 31.5 hours per week (range: 2–65 hours). In those households with more than one adult, a

TABLE 2.4
Age of Children with Special Needs in Study Group

AGE IN YEARS	% OF GROUP	n
1	4.3	4
2	6.5	6
3	5.4	5
4	9.8	9
5	7.6	7
6	3.3	3
7	12.0	11
8	1.1	1
9	6.5	6
10	2.2	2
11	8.7	8
12	7.6	7
13	1.1	1
14	2.2	2
15	6.5	6
16	3.3	3
17	3.3	3
18	5.4	5
19	1.1	1
20	1.1	1
31	1.1	1

second adult worked outside of the home 74% of the time for an average of 43.6 hours a week (range: 10–80 hours).

The average child with specialized needs in the study was just over 9 years old. As Table 2.4 shows, the children were relatively evenly distributed across the age range of 1 to 18 years of age. Three adults were also identified for the study. Two of these individuals were still covered by the special education law in their state and so were in school, and the third was a 31-year-old who had always lived at home. This person was not identified to the project director until all of the data was collected and initial processing had begun. Because of the substantial resources already expended on collecting and processing the data on this family, we decided to retain them in the study group.

The study group was made up of almost twice as many males (64.1%, $n = 59$) as females (34.8%, $n = 32$). (For one subject, sex was not identified.)

Just over half of the families (54.3%, $n = 50$) indicated that the child's disability was identified at birth or shortly thereafter. A total of 81.5% were diagnosed by 6 years. Eight members of the study group (8.8%) were either injured, became ill, or were diagnosed during their adolescent years (5 respondents did not complete this item). Ten children have a disability as the result of an accident: automotive (5), near drowning (3), or fall (2).

TABLE 2.5
Percentage of Study Group with Various Disabling Conditions

CONDITION	% PRIMARY DIAGNOSIS	% SECONDARY DIAGNOSIS[a]
Other	15.2	27.2
Cerebral palsy	10.9	8.7
Mental retardation: profound	8.7	8.7
Emotional disturbance	6.5	6.5
Traumatic brain injury	6.5	1.1
Birth defects	5.4	6.5
Spina bifida	5.4	—
Cystic fibrosis	5.4	—
Heart disease	4.3	2.2
Asthma	3.3	6.5
Autism	3.3	3.3
Metabolic disorder	3.3	2.2
Hemophilia	3.3	1.1
Epilepsy	2.2	16.3
Orthopedic impairment	2.2	13.1
Stroke	2.2	1.1
Diabetes	2.2	—
Spinal cord injury	2.2	—
Mental retardation: moderate	1.1	3.3
Muscular dystrophy	1.1	—
Bronchopulmonary dysplasia	1.1	—
Neuromuscular disease	1.1	—
Tuberous sclerosis	1.1	—
Amputation	1.1	—
Sickle cell anemia	1.1	—
Learning disability	—	6.5
Kidney disease	—	3.3
Visual impairment	—	3.3
Hearing impairment	—	2.2
Cancer	—	1.1
Leukemia	—	1.1

[a] 63 Informants identified one or more secondary diagnoses, 33 identified at least 2, and 19 indicated 3 or more.

A majority of the families indicated that their children had complex medical or psychological histories that led, in 69% of the cases, to multiple diagnoses. The specialized nature of the children in this group is captured by the figures presented in Table 2.5. As a result of our efforts to sample a diverse group of families, the diagnoses listed here have very small percentages associated with them, and the largest single diagnostic category is "Other." This reflects the fact that many of the children in this group represent people who have some of the very lowest incidence, rare disorders, including such conditions as Ondine's curse, trisomy 13 syndrome, Rett syndrome, Pterygeium syndrome, neurofibromatosis, Crohn's disease, and others.

These descriptive statistics give some picture of the families and children we are talking about, but real understanding only emerges as we listen to the descriptions provided by the parents and the interviewers. These six examples, one from each of the groupings we used to guide identification of study group participants, present a picture of the lives of these families.

On April 10, 1988, Fred was involved in a severe auto accident. We didn't think he would live. He has an enclosed head injury—traumatic brain injury. Right side was paralyzed. Shoulder and collar bone abducted. Also his walking is abnormal. Right hand will not close—drops things. Kidney problems from accident. Has some seizures due to accident. Main thing for Fred is the emotional upset, for which he's getting counseling. His abnormal walk and little feeling on the right side make him unhappy. (AR05)

He has spina bifida. Mom noticed "open hole" on his back at birth. Father asked, "What's wrong here?" Doctor was blunt and callous, said, "Don't start crying now. You'll have much more to cry about later." Jeff proved everyone wrong! They said he'd be severely retarded and couldn't do anything but be a vegetable. He's done so well! (NY06)

When he was 8 or 9 years old, Bill was having problems 5 times a week in school. So he was placed in special education as severely emotionally disturbed. He slapped a teacher early last year for trying to take him to a time-out period. He did it again to an aide. He also threatened teacher verbally: "I'm going to kill you." Was put under court probation. About 4th grade he was measured to have a "low I.Q." whereas before that the school said he was "bright."

In the evening it gets bad from time to time. Other people have to keep him busy because he gets restless. Last night, for example, he took a knife and threatened mother. Mother does not understand her son. She feels threatened at home. Various attempts at counseling have not been effective as far as mother is concerned. To her the counseling has been more of a monitoring system. Now she feels like a battered parent. (CA05)

At 2½ they thought it was a visual problem—would fall and trip. She was diagnosed with ceroid lipofuscinosis. Eventually all organs will be involved; brain cells are dying. Cannot see—lungs are having difficulty. Cannot walk or talk because of brain cells. Disease will get to brain stem and she will die. They live in a 2 story/4 bedrooms. They have turned dining room into her bedroom, added water bed, to include child and make her part of family. Not feasible to house her upstairs and not involved in downstairs. Feeding pump, oxygen concentrator, suction pump, mobility unit—everything must be portable. (MI04)

At about 6 months he cried continually with pain in his stomach and then they noticed his hands and foot were swollen. The swelling didn't go down. He was referred to the hospital where he was diagnosed as having sickle cell anemia. It is associated with pain in hands, joints, and stomach, and lack of fluids, and too much exercise can bring on an episode which causes hospitalization. Also, if he gets cold, it can bring on pain—pneumonia can be a side effect of the disease. His condition and lifestyle have to be monitored constantly as a preventative method as well as to detect early symptoms of a sickle cell episode. (FL04)

At 3 days, she got into respiratory distress, transferred her to the neonatal unit and they did surgery to correct the hernia. There followed a whole series of surgeries and she was trached when she was 18 months. Now, the entire esophagus is damaged, and they can't do anything about it. In the end of 1982 she became ventilator dependent. Then she has had ups and downs ever since.

Nonetheless Esther has been home on a ventilator for 6 years. She is a pioneer in all aspects. One of the first children to come home on a vent in this part of the state. She's mainstreamed into the classroom. The county has fought every service Esther has needed and Mom has been a terrific advocate for herself and Esther. Dad walked out very early on. He lives in the same town and has no contact. Esther is surrounded by love and care because of Mom's inner strength and calm. (NY14)

The Daily Routine

A picture of the level of care that these families must provide for their children emerges when we ask them to describe the daily routine in the home. Here the emphasis is solely on the amount of support the children need in the regular activities of daily life, not on any specialized care that may be required because of their condition. This functional measure of the child's level of disability or level of assistance as it relates to 10 activities of everyday life and a global measure of overall assistance needed are summarized in Table 2.6.

As can be seen in Table 2.6, when we asked the caregiver to describe the degree of assistance the child needed during various activities of the day, the response for "extensive assistance" was in the range of 27–65% of the respondents. The low end of this range is associated with "Communicating," where the need for complete supervision dropped to 27.2% of the cases. On the other extreme, 65.2% of the children are perceived as

TABLE 2.6
Levels of Assistance Needed in Daily Living Activities

ACTIVITY AREA	% OF STUDY GROUP REQUIRING[a]		
	NO ASSISTANCE	MODERATE ASSISTANCE	EXTENSIVE ASSISTANCE
Toileting	41.3	7.6	48.9
Eating and drinking	43.5	13.0	41.3
Bathing	29.3	18.5	50.0
Grooming	32.6	14.1	50.0
Dressing	34.8	17.4	43.5
Communicating	48.9	17.4	27.2
Play	27.2	34.8	33.7
Movement in home	43.5	15.2	38.0
Movement in community	20.7	9.8	65.2
Changing position	28.3	6.5	33.7
Medical monitoring	8.7	21.7	51.1
Overall	17.4	26.1	54.3

[a] All rows do not total to 100% because of missing responses.

needing extensive aid or supervision when they venture out into the community. More than half of the children were reported to need an extensive level of medical monitoring due to their disability or medical condition. When caregivers were asked to rate the overall care needs of the child, 54.3% described them as "extensive," the extreme rating on our scale.

A final measure of the day-to-day demands of care faced by these families can be found in the degree to which they find their sleep interrupted by the nighttime care of the child. A total of 32.6% ($n = 30$) of the informants said that the child did not sleep through the night on a regular basis. The majority of this group ($n = 20$) said this was not just a minor sleep disruption and was a cause for concern.

When we asked them to rate the care demands of the child against their expectation at diagnosis, 29.3% of the caregivers said the demands of care were much higher than they expected at the time they brought their child home. When asked to identify the period of the day which places the most demands on them, 18.5% of caregivers identified the morning and 6.5% of them said "constant;" 32.6% of the respondents said that no period of the day was more demanding than any other. However, when this last response is reviewed in light of information gained in the rest of the interview the "no period more demanding" response seems, in many cases, to indicate a "constant" high level of care.

> There's not a most difficult time—I have a routine. Paul's daily schedule is so routine now to me that this question doesn't seem to apply. I can't think of a response. (VA01)

A "constant, high level of care" is a very sterile measure on a Leikert scale. The reality in the lives of the families in the study group is something else. As the selected summaries presented here indicate, many of these families are engaged in the hard work of personal care for most of their waking day.

> Mike has to be changed 5 to 10 times per day depending on his bowel movement. Sometimes he has very loose stools and has several bowel movements a day. There was a two year period Mike had an ileostomy that has since been repaired. There are periods of constipation which require stimulation. I'm [Mother] the only one doing this stuff. Mike is fed by gastrostomy tube with a feeding machine. He is fed 230 cc 5× a day. Each feeding takes one hour. He gets a bath every day. He is submerged in a baby bath tub that is set down in a big bathtub so he hangs out both ends of the small tub. He weighs 60 lbs. of dead weight and is very difficult to bathe. Sometimes he has to be bathed twice per day, depending on bowel movement or if his gastrostomy tube has leaked.
>
> Mike sleeps when he wants to, mostly during the day. He sleeps with a heart monitor on which alarms several times per night, because he stops breathing frequently. Usually I'm up by 8:00 and often cannot go to bed until 12:00 or 1:00 because of Mike's feedings, medications. It's hard to fit all of this into a day and still have time for sleep. (AR11)

For those families whose children do not require intensive ongoing physical care, the demands of daily care are also intense. For some, the major cost of care is the disappearance of the normal routines most people count on to organize their lives.

> At night he has this terrible energy—medication has not controlled his energy level. His bouncing and running behavior might keep the family up all night. He is also subject to "night terrors"—a specific type of nightmare which causes him to scream in terror, sometimes throughout the night. I'm not sure how aware Todd is of what he's going through. Some nights he never goes to sleep. He might appear in his parents' bedroom and just start talking about some topic of interest to him or bounce and run through the house. (VA06)

For other families, the daily requirements of care may not be all consuming but often entail constant attention to detail.

> Franco can do all his self care without any help. However, he can't be left alone because he is not focused and has difficulty following directions. I have to design his free time and write down what he has to do. He can't

follow more than two or three instructions. If he were left to his own devices he'd live like an animal. (CA10)

Mother just has to make sure that Mary gets snacks mid-morning (10:00) and mid-afternoon (2:30) because her blood sugar drops at these times of day and she needs the snacks to bring sugar level to where it's safe. Mother says she has to monitor Mary all of the time because of her diabetic condition. For Mary to get a cold is a big deal. Because of the severity of Mary's diabetic condition, all "normal" infections, viruses, etc., that a child gets are further compounded because of the diabetes. If she gets a cut, it has to be watched because it could so easily turn into something serious. The mother states that she daily checks Mary for cuts, bruises, etc. (FL06)

Of course, this need to maintain a heightened level of awareness brings with it a cost that is often at least as profound as carrying and lifting all day.

She just needs someone to be around to monitor and in case something happens. Doctors told family, "Don't treat her like a cardiac cripple." But the father highlighted what it meant to be constantly on the alert for what could happen: "Sometimes I couldn't go to sleep—my eyes would stay open." (MN08)

When asked how they managed to maintain their level of effort and their energy, most parents are practical—they develop a regular routine for their lives—and more than a little stoic.

We always thought we can't allow ourselves to have expectations—the most you can do is maintain. Given no expectations, so have we none. At first, it was a lot of work. Now, it's a part of daily life. It's like brushing your teeth—need to do it. (MN03)

Taking Care of the Child

The extensive questions dealing with the exact nature of the child's specialized care fall into four categories: (a) medication administration; (b) medical monitoring procedures; (c) specialized treatments or procedures that are performed on a regular basis; and (d) challenging behaviors and behavioral interventions. These *specialized* activities, which are in addition to the regular supports provided to the children described in the previous section, are summarized in Tables 2.7, 2.8, 2.9, and 2.10. Merely totalling the numbers of procedures, treatments, and therapies most of these families perform affirms the "extensive" care needs of 54% of these children. This is further underscored by the fact that 45.6% of the families reported that they perform some specialized clinical monitoring of their child on at least a daily basis. Fully 22.8% of the families summarized the care of their child by saying he or she needs 24 hour a day monitoring.

As outlined in Table 2.7, the majority of the children received some form of medication on a regular basis. The majority of these medications were given at least daily using the full gamut of possible modes of administration. In all cases medications were administered at least some of the time by the parents. Anywhere from 20% to 85.7% of the parents reported difficulty with particular modes of administration.

Just as parents take responsibility for every possible mode of administering medication, they also perform a wide array of medical monitoring procedures. It is not surprising to find that individuals with the disabilities and medical conditions found in our study group need the amount of monitoring outlined in Table 2.8 on a regular basis. What is illuminating is the frequency with which some relatively specialized procedures are performed by parents or other family members rather than by professionals.

Table 2.9 describes the extensive array of specialized procedures and treatment that members of the study group received regularly. Here again, a parent or family member performed most of these procedures the majority of the time.

> I have to constantly monitor Tim for any development of viruses because the medication that Tim takes has a diuretic in it and he easily dehydrates—it usually means hospitalization. He has the continuous feeder at night plus four times a day and breathing treatment three times a day. Need to regularly change dressing on G-tube. Tim takes three medications plus breathing treatment. All four given daily. Temperature, pulse, respiration must be monitored. At night put on oxygen machine to help monitor amount of oxygen being received because parents are asleep. During the day I monitor it. (FL01)

> Respiratory therapy three times a day normally. When sick or congested, 4–5 times a day, plus medications. She takes 11 different medications, including 5 vitamins. Need to monitor stool samples daily—make sure they are solid. The inhalation therapy is not disturbing, but when we're both tired it's no fun—sometimes it's a bother. Takes a half hour—15 minutes on mask, 15 minutes pounding. It depends on her mood—if she's tired at night, she'll sleep through it. Sometimes she'll fight all the way. (MN03)

> Giving medication on time, right dosage, watching for fatigue, stool color change, change in seizures—hard to just be Mom. (WA10)

A significant number of the children in our study group also presented some form of behavioral difficulty. Thirty-eight members of the study group

TABLE 2.7
Types of Medication Administration Required

MODE OF ADMINISTRATION	LESS THAN WEEKLY	AT LEAST WEEKLY	1 OR 2Xs DAILY	AT LEAST 3Xs DAILY	AS NEEDED	ROW TOTAL	% REPORTING DIFFICULTY
Topically	—	3.3	2.2	4.3	2.2	12.0	27.3
Orally	1.1	3.3	25.0	20.7	2.2	52.3	21.3
Rectally	—	1.1	4.4	1.1	—	6.6	66.7
Injection	2.2	1.1	2.2	—	3.3	8.8	85.7
Intravenously	1.1	1.1	—	1.1	3.3	6.6	33.0
Via G-Tube	—	—	4.4	10.9	—	15.3	35.7
Other modes	—	—	4.4	4.4	2.2	11.0	20.0

% OF STUDY GROUP REQUIRING

TABLE 2.8
Medical Monitoring Procedures Required

MONITORING PROCEDURE	LESS THAN WEEKLY	% OF STUDY GROUP REQUIRING			AS NEEDED	ROW TOTAL	% FAMILY PERFORMED
		AT LEAST WEEKLY	1 OR 2Xs DAILY	AT LEAST 3Xs DAILY			
Weight	18.5	7.6	3.3	2.2	—	31.6	37.9
Temperature	6.5	3.3	14.1	5.4	1.1	30.4	66.7
Blood sample	20.7	2.2	3.3	1.1	—	27.3	20.8
Respiration	2.2	1.1	15.2	7.6	1.1	27.2	68.0
Pulse	5.4	2.2	13.0	5.4	—	26.0	47.8
Urine sample	12.0	4.3	5.4	—	—	21.7	52.6
Blood pressure	6.5	2.2	9.8	—	1.1	19.6	33.3
Other	7.6	3.3	2.2	2.2	1.1	16.4	54.6
Liquid intake/output	1.1	2.2	5.4	6.5	—	15.2	62.5
Stool sample	9.8	1.1	3.3	—	—	14.2	53.9

TABLE 2.9
Specialized Treatments and Procedures Required

TREATMENT OR PROCEDURE	LESS THAN WEEKLY	AT LEAST WEEKLY	DAILY	TWICE DAILY	EVERY 4 HOURS	EVERY 2 HOURS	CONSTANT	AS NEEDED	ROW TOTAL	% FAMILY PERFORMED
Other procedures	2.2	9.8	4.3	1.1	6.5	1.1	7.6	3.3	35.9	48.8
Other physical therapy	—	18.5	7.6	2.2	1.1	—	—	—	29.4	27.5
Skin care	4.3	—	8.7	3.3	2.2	4.3	4.3	—	27.1	75.0
Range of motion	—	5.4	9.8	4.3	4.3	1.1	1.1	—	26.0	50.0
Blood levels	18.5	1.1	—	—	—	—	—	—	19.6	20.0
Monitor vital signs	—	—	5.4	2.2	3.3	1.1	6.5	1.1	19.6	53.6
Gastrostomy	1.1	—	2.2	1.1	7.6	2.2	3.3	—	17.5	60.0
Tracheostomy care	—	1.1	3.3	1.1	2.2	3.3	5.4	—	16.4	53.9
Positioning	—	—	1.1	—	3.3	9.8	—	1.1	15.3	64.3
Sterile dressings	1.1	—	3.3	3.3	3.3	—	1.1	1.1	13.2	61.9
Dental care	2.2	1.1	2.2	5.4	2.2	—	—	—	13.1	60.0
Postural drainage	—	1.1	—	3.3	4.3	3.3	1.1	—	13.1	60.0
Oxygen administration	2.2	—	1.1	—	1.1	—	7.6	1.1	13.1	58.8
Inhalation therapy	—	—	—	2.2	6.5	1.1	1.1	2.2	13.1	61.1
Enemas	2.2	4.3	2.2	1.1	—	—	—	3.3	13.1	68.8
Foot care	—	2.2	3.3	2.2	1.1	—	1.1	—	9.9	90.0
Oral/nasal suctioning	—	—	1.1	—	1.1	1.1	4.3	1.1	8.7	63.6
Eye care	2.2	1.1	1.1	1.1	1.1	1.1	—	—	6.6	66.7
Blood sugar test	2.2	—	—	1.1	1.1	—	—	1.1	5.5	66.7
Ear irrigation	2.2	—	—	1.1	1.1	—	—	—	4.4	66.7
Parenteral feeding	1.1	1.1	—	—	1.1	—	—	—	3.3	33.3
Nasal gastric feeding	—	—	1.1	—	—	—	—	—	1.1	100.0

(41.3%) stated that their child exhibited some form of "challenging behavior," and 65.8% of that number ($n = 25$) had sought help outside the home in dealing with that behavior. Table 2.10 displays the frequency of behaviors and interventions being dealt with by this latter group. Of the interventions implemented by the family and recorded in Table 2.10, 35% were "low intensity," 30% were "medium intensity," and 35% were "high intensity interventions." Additionally, 20.5% of the behavior intervention group ($n = 9$) were receiving medication specifically for their behavior.

Another measure of the children's extensive care needs is the inventory of specialized equipment in many of their homes. The majority of families (53.3%) reported the presence of such equipment. While in many cases this represented only an item or two, some families supplied extensive lists of equipment. For families with children on oxygen, "specialized equipment" included such things as running tubing throughout their home so the child would not be restricted within the house. Of families with equipment, 25.1% reported problems with monitoring it, and 34.8% reported problems in getting service.

Frequent crises contribute to the tension with which these families live. The majority of the families (53.3%, $n = 49$) reported that within the last month their child had experienced some sort of crisis which required an extraordinary intervention. For 71.4% ($n = 35$) of the families, the extraordinary event required more than 5 hours of activity. Eighty-four percent of families reported that this level of extraordinary intervention was typical for them. For 27 families (55.1%), this extraordinary event required at least one visit to a physician or emergency room. Ten families had three or more such visits in one month. One family had eight unplanned medical encounters. Again, this pattern was reported as fairly typical by the majority of the families with unplanned medical encounters (79.6%).

For some families, the simplest of daily activities becomes a potential threat to the welfare of their child, so their daily routine becomes transformed into "specialized care."

> There is a monitor when Jacob is in bathtub, etc., to see that he doesn't slip and fall which could start bleeding. Or if he does, so that they will know what to do immediately. Usually pressure and ice is applied. If bleeding continues an injection of "Factor 8," which is to control bleeding, is given.

> He must be monitored where he plays, e.g., no glass, sharp edges on things, etc. Any kind of cut or fall could affect Jacob's condition. The living area of Jacob's home is almost barrier free. All furniture has been built or rebuilt by the father with rounded edges. The parents state that they didn't take training wheels off bicycle for Jake for one year after he had the bike for fear he might fall. The mother states that when he rides it now she

TABLE 2.10
Occurrences of Challenging Behaviors and Behavioral Interventions

BEHAVIOR	LESS THAN MONTHLY	1–3Xs A MONTH	MORE THAN WEEKLY	MORE THAN DAILY	HOURLY	ROW TOTAL
Self-injurious behavior						
Frequency	1.1	1.1	3.3	9.8	1.1	16.4
Frequency of intervention	1.1	2.2	4.3	8.7	—	16.3
Repetitive (stereotypic) behavior						
Frequency	1.1	2.2	1.1	9.8	2.2	16.4
Frequency of intervention	5.4	1.1	1.1	9.8	2.2	19.6
Withdrawal						
Frequency	2.2	—	2.2	5.4	—	9.8
Frequency of intervention	4.3	—	2.2	4.3	1.1	11.9
Harmful to others						
Frequency	1.1	1.1	1.1	5.4	1.1	9.8
Frequency of intervention	2.2	1.1	2.2	3.3	1.1	9.8
Socially offensive behaviors						
Frequency	—	1.1	2.2	8.7	2.2	14.2
Frequency of intervention	2.2	—	3.3	7.6	1.1	14.2
Destruction of property						
Frequency	—	2.2	3.3	2.2	1.1	8.8
Frequency of intervention	2.2	3.3	3.3	2.2	—	11.0
Stealing or hoarding						
Frequency	2.2	—	—	2.2	—	4.4
Frequency of intervention	3.3	1.1	—	1.1	—	5.5
Wandering						
Frequency	1.1	1.1	1.1	5.4	1.1	9.8
Frequency of intervention	2.2	—	2.2	5.4	1.1	10.9
Other behavioral or social/emotional difficulties						
Frequency	—	—	1.1	2.2	1.1	4.4
Frequency of intervention	—	—	2.2	2.2	—	4.4

watches him. The doctor says the main thing is to protect his head. Any head injury could result in bleeding internally and you wouldn't always know this. (FL09)

All of the preparations and precautions notwithstanding, crises can be brought on by anything.

We're used to it all—we got routines down. The longer we do it, the smoother things go . . . Only one scary time so far—Douglas's tube caught on the door handle and his trach came out. I panicked, but Douglas's father was home and he "simply" reinserted the trach and reattached the tube to the ventilator machine. Douglas meanwhile had turned gray, then blue for just a minute or less. I was crying as he began breathing again and his color came back. Douglas said to me, "Are you OK, Mom?" I don't think he has a recollection of what's happened at those moments when his breathing stopped. (VA03)

For some families, the day-to-day care of the child has transformed them into such experts that they did not report as crises some events which our interviewers classified as life threatening.

He can aspirate, so meals must be organized. Two months ago he was yelling and he choked on rice. He went out and I had to bag him and change his trach. When I did there was a rice plug, and a new law of quiet and calm was set down for meal times. (NY07)

Another factor which complicates the lives of these families is the loss of privacy they experience as a constant parade of outsiders tramp through their homes.

Nursing care is around the clock Monday through Friday afternoon and weekend nights (hired nurses). Weekend days and every other Friday and Sunday night it is just us. (VA08)

The situation facing Pete's family sums up the anxiety and tension that can become just a regular part of life for these families.

Pete requires constant skilled care and continuous 24-hour monitoring (according to individualized criteria including behavior, coordination, cognitive function, level of activity, physical findings). His clinical condition is highly unstable and influenced by weather, fatigue, activity, etc. He has sudden episodes of severe wheezing and active distress and has required emergency resuscitative care on several occasions during the past year. We have confronted (1) choking episode on solid food, loss of consciousness—Heimlich maneuver. Successful within 1 minute—at bedside all night watching for sudden onset of respiratory distress on MD's advice (severe episode, complete obstruction). (2) Midnight asthma attack—

TABLE 2.11
Impact of Disability on Household

TYPE OF IMPACT	% HOUSEHOLDS
Major change in family lifestyle	89.1
Significant impact on siblings	72.8
Decision on where to live influenced	63.0
Major increase in household expenses	56.5
Someone gave up a job	50.0
Need to make physical adaptations	43.5
Someone did not pursue employment	43.5
Someone did not pursue further education	37.0
Someone refused a transfer or promotion	21.7
Job change for better hours	15.2
Job change for better medical coverage	7.6

severe—minimal BS cyanosis—responded to 40% oxygen, Alupent mist IV aminophylline drip—all-nighter. (3) A milder asthmatic attack requiring additional meds or Alupent mist—total time 4 hours. (4) Viral gastroenteritis, fever 102, danger of aspiration from vomiting while asleep—more all-nighters. (NY15)

Being a Family

From the interviews, it was clear that the major challenge confronting most of the families in our study group was how to meet the often complex care needs of their child with a disability or chronic health problem and still function as a family. One series of interview items attempted to gain some sense of how the demands of home care affected the family's daily life. In this area it is really impossible to separate the answers to the survey items from the interviews. Each family has a unique story, and the survey items provided a forum for interviewees to describe their experiences in caring for their child. It is in this area that the interview data are the richest.

Perhaps the greatest measure of the impact of the child's disability on the family is the extent to which the child must physically leave the home either on a short-term or long-term basis because of the child's care needs. In the study group, 17.4% of the children had been placed out of the home at some time, and 21.7% of the families had at least considered out-of-home placement, indicating the extent of pressures on the families.

Table 2.11 summarizes a group of what might be called the opportunity costs associated with home care: major changes in life-style, physical environment, daily routine, or opportunities for personal development that have been influenced by the care needs of the child with special needs. In reviewing the families' comments that accompanied their responses to the list of opportunity costs, it was evident that the list of categories, although useful to the researcher, did not capture the global impact which the child's needs have on the family.

> We moved from Burnsville to Bloomington because of school district—lost friends—didn't go to church for several years—wouldn't let him stay in church nursery—would choke and gag—people were afraid. Couldn't drive on freeway—he wouldn't stay in car seat—had to take back roads and stop all the time. Didn't have baby-sitters—went from being socially active to hermits—lose a whole lot emotionally. My husband was offered a job and turned it down—we didn't dare leave. Couldn't take a vacation—lost freedom to make some choices in our life. (MN02)

> Decided not to have a third child. Decided to stay here in this town because of services. We have met wonderful people—parents of kids with disabilities. Wonderful teachers, assistants, resource people. We all grew up in ways we didn't want to. (NY04)

An example of opportunity cost is seen in the 63% of respondents who said their child's disability had affected where the family lived. When we look at the interview follow-up to this question, we find this effect took three forms: (a) some families consciously chose to live in an area where they thought there were good services, (b) some families chose to live in a neighborhood close to a hospital or clinic which would treat their child, and (c) many families found the expenses associated with the care of their child either made it impossible for them to move into the kind of housing they wanted or forced them to sell a home and live in an apartment or less expensive house. As in the case of the family below, merely saying the child's disability influenced where the family lives hardly captures the reality behind that statement.

> They live in a 2-bedroom brick rented home. In general, the area is pretty run down. Most residents moved from the area due to a chemical spill. For them, it's close to the hospital and doctors' offices. They continue to live there because they can't afford to move and it is close to the services their son needs. (AR09)

The transformation that the families experienced usually began at birth or shortly thereafter when the child's condition became evident. Families told very similar stories of being overwhelmed by the experience, which was often intensified by the hospital atmosphere and the demeanor of the professionals at birth. Many families reported that professionals dealt with them in a cold, detached manner which contributed to the confusion they were already feeling. Some recounted a sense that they were to blame for their child's condition, or even direct accusations. In addition, the attitude of the immediate and extended family was often formed by this initial negative experience, and in many cases, the family changed its attitude toward the child later—but not always.

Once the initial shock was dealt with and the decision was made to care for the child at home, most of the families were totally unprepared for the radical changes that followed. Families typically responded to the inquiries in this area with an inventory of physical, social, and psychological changes associated with the care of their child.

> I [Dad] can write a book on it [the changes in their life]—you lose all flexibility. The brother didn't have a normal 3rd and 4th year of childhood. He spent it in the hospital with his brother and he is very sensitive. The parents try to compensate. The family gets separated because they can't just get in the van and go. No spontaneity. Brother is too young but is starting to know the names of certain equipment and can help in a pinch. He often wants to just stay home with his brother. Mom can't seek outside employment because of Jim. Mom had to drop out of school. We are moving back to the city to be closer to the hospital—moving closer to friends, family and support. We cannot think about having another child. Jim is at home. Jim is striving towards being a typical kid—his brother loves him and is so glad he is home. Jim is happy and so adjusted. Mom feels all this made her a stronger person. It made our marriage stronger. Jim is a joy. Made the priorities clear—life is better defined. (NY11)

Particularly noteworthy in this excerpt is the emphasis on how Jim's needs have had an effect on his brother. This was a special area of concern in every case where the child with special care needs had siblings.

The extensive list of disabilities, complex care needs, daily crises, effects on family lifestyle, and other factors related to providing home care that we have reviewed thus far present powerful data. No family exposed to these forces can avoid profound stress and major changes. Yet these findings are somewhat deceptive. What is missing is some measure of the positive results of the family's decision to care for the child at home. This positive impact comes through only when we listen to the parents' stories.

> *Dad:* Biggest thing is becoming acquainted with entirely different set of folks who share similar things. I head a parent group that meets monthly, publishes newsletter. Now I better appreciate the normal development of our other child. Lots of intangible goods that come out of seeing DD child develop.

> *Mom:* Robbie truly a blessing. People in our lives because of Robbie are people we learn from, are inspired by: teachers, medical people, other professionals, parents—expanded our horizon. Less afraid, more understanding of people with disabilities. Made clear to them that this was bigger than them. As things worked out I couldn't be happier. None of this could be possible if he was placed out of home. Expanded our connection to community around us. Have had to reach outside of ourselves: joined

church, parents group of disabled, spiritually connected to family of man, became active politically, children's initiative. (WA09)

The majority of families spoke of the sense of accomplishment they had gained from seeing and contributing to their child's growth and development. Even in the cases of children with degenerative conditions or complex medical needs, parents reported a real sense of achievement in meeting the child's needs within the family and an emerging awareness of their own capacity and competence as parents. When we probed for less concrete outcomes of home care, we heard the families talk about getting to know their child as a person, seeing him or her as a contributing member of the family, experiencing a sense of togetherness and a growing sense of personal strength, reordering their priorities in life, siblings learning about being caring people, and other factors that are not as easily quantified as the special interventions that are needed.

Many of the parents, particularly the mothers, noted that the whole experience of fighting for their child totally reordered their value system and gave them a very different perspective on their own competence.

> I grew up—learned and developed patience, tolerance. Now I have a different outlook on life—to face each day, whatever it brings with it. Mary and I have gone through some real crises and that has brought us closer. (FL06)

> I devote a tremendous amount of time in meetings and advocating for my child—about 180 hours a month. (CA10)

> The mother says she has gained a different sense of what's important. Generally speaking she says she lives in the present. While some parents live in the future, she takes one day at a time. It makes you realize your own mortality. She states she's really glad she's George's mother and her boys are what makes life worth living. (FL05)

> Mostly that it opens your eyes on restrictions on the disabled. Makes you aware of how society is geared against them. It opens your eyes to other people—makes you sensitive. In some ways it's hard but in some ways it's good for the ego. I can say I did it. (NY18)

The following excerpts from the interview with Pete's adoptive mother testify to the joy of seeing the child as a child—a unique, growing, human being. It is clear from this and many other interviews that it is this awareness that gives the families the strength to endure all they must confront.

> Most stress and dissatisfaction come from outside sources. Pete has been a joy (despite his problems), and I have never regretted my decision to

adopt him. I have learned (and I am still learning) from him everyday, both as a professional and as a mother. Pete's excitement about life and learning despite his severe problems, despite his past, is remarkable. His achievements, emotionally, academically, artistically over the past 3 years are amazing, considering his hospitalization in the ICU for 4½ years. Best of all Pete is a funny, bright, loving child who gets into lots of mischief to keep me busy, but who constantly makes me laugh (often at ourselves). Pete has enriched our family in a way that no one else could, and each of us has learned something about ourselves through him. Not one of us would trade a single hour with Pete for a winning lottery ticket. We're all very proud of him. Pete is the most loved member of his immediate and his extended family. (NY15)

Family, Friends, and Neighbors

In the family support literature there is increasing discussion of the importance of building on supports that already exist in local communities. With this in mind, we felt that it was important to get some measure of how this informal system supported the families in the study group. The responses to these survey questions indicated that most of the families had a relatively shallow informal system of support. Specifically, 30.4% said they got no assistance from a relative outside the household, 32.6% said they got no help from any nonprofessional outside the household, and 16.3% said they had no one to turn to for aid even in a time of crisis.

> Former friends in the neighborhood have abandoned us and don't associate with her anymore. Some of the neighbors think her condition could be infectious. (CA03)

> Grandma feels there is no one to turn to. She is case manager—does hiring, firing, scheduling herself—very isolated, very independent. If something happened to Grandma, he would go to hospital. (WA02)

Unfortunately, in many cases the primary caregiver told of instances in which other family members were not able to accept the child with specialized needs or were resistant to the idea of home care. In several cases where this situation led to divorce, the informants indicated that the relationship had been headed in that direction and the added pressures associated with the child's needs only hastened the inevitable. In most cases, the responses to our inquiries in this area were short and without much elaboration.

> The whole family pulled away due to long-term prognosis. There was a lot of pressure to put him away. (MI07)

While essentially every family told at least one tale of callousness, neglect, obfuscation, or arrogance on the part of professionals, many reported long-term relationships that go far beyond the limits of the job description. It is little wonder families identified these professionals as some of the people they can depend on as "informal" supports.

> Best doctor she could get. Doctor would drive approximately 30 miles just to see Suzie. Very supportive and understanding. Helps out more than could ever ask. Checks in on Suzie without having reason. (AR09)

When it came to the rather intangible quality of the psychological sense of community, the members of the study group did not feel particularly well connected to their communities and neighborhoods: 13% felt very isolated from their neighborhood, and another 30.4% felt somewhat isolated. In general, the interviews indicated that this sense of isolation could be at least partially attributed to the fact that many children were in segregated education programs not centered in the local community. A number of the interviewees suggested that separate special education facilities left their children with no neighborhood friends or led friends that they had made to shun them. In almost every case, the families indicated a sense of being the outsider. This feeling of isolation coupled with the time demands associated with the care of their children leaves little energy or motivation for connecting with their communities. In some instances, neighbors were actively hostile.

> People wouldn't answer door. He was hit on head with rock and went to hospital—neighbors called to say he deserved it because he's a bad kid. (MN02)

On the other hand, as noted above, some families had become members of very supportive networks of parents and advocates not attached to their place of residence. Several interviewees spoke of extensive support and social networks that had grown up in their larger community around the needs of their child.

> During the outdoor interview in the yard, Tina interacted with her two children, an older child's boyfriend, her sister, her sister's toddler and infant, her sister's husband, and her mother. With each of these people she was supportive and warm (the yard was eventually filled with people). Tina seems to be a mainstay of the extended family. (NY02)

Paying the Bills

Table 2.12 provides a summary of the various sources of funds the families used to cover the expenses related to the care of their child with

TABLE 2.12

Sources of Funds for Meeting Costs of Care

SOURCE OF FUNDS	FAMILIES USING %	n
Private insurance	62.0	57
Public health insurance	43.5	40
SSI	17.4	16
Out of pocket	59.8	55
Savings	22.8	21
Sale of assets	7.6	7
Other means	42.4	39

a disability or special health care need. Because of the range of costs that families encountered, no one source of income covered the cost for any family. On average, each family used two or three of the sources outlined. State family support programs, the major focus of this monograph, fall into the "other" category, along with local charities, not-for-profit agencies, and financial aid from family and friends. Of the 42.4% of families who indicated "other source of funds," 27.2% reported that they received some form of financial assistance from state family support programs and other sources to aid them in meeting the costs of care.

For families who were dependent on Medicaid and other forms of public assistance to cover the cost of care, maintenance of program eligibility was consistently reported as a major family concern. Retaining eligibility, in turn, affected the family's life style. In fact, 12% of the families indicate they have had to "spend down" or otherwise divest themselves of resources in order to qualify for assistance. These families were not just affected by the demands and the out-of-pocket cost of care, but they also had to keep the family income at an artificially low level for fear of losing much needed Medicaid coverage. In this regard, it is worth noting that 13% of the children with disabilities had been without any form of medical coverage for periods of time ranging from 1 month to 8 years (average 16.4 months), and 17.4% of their families had lacked coverage for an average period of 1 year. One family, not included in our average, had never had any type of medical coverage.

Table 2.13 summarizes the families' experiences in filing claims against their medical insurance carrier. About 45% of the families reported that significant aspects of home care were not covered by their insurance. The 45 families who were able to provide us with detailed information had filed a total of 2,340 claims in the year preceding the interview. The average number of claims filed per family was 52 (range 2–250). Forty-one families

TABLE 2.13

Insurance Coverage of Services

SERVICE	% OF HOUSEHOLDS COVERED	NOT COVERED
Medication	75.0	4.3
Physician visits	72.8	1.1
Hospitalization	67.4	3.3
Medical procedures	57.6	1.1
Durable medical equipment	44.6	16.3
Specialist consultation	38.0	14.3
Habilitative treatments	27.2	4.3
Home care (nursing, etc.)	25.0	12.1
Adaptive equipment	23.9	3.3
Equipment maintenance	16.3	1.1
Diapers	12.0	8.8
Transportation	10.9	4.3
Other	9.8	17.6
Specialized diets	8.7	4.3
Out of town travel	3.3	1.1
Home/vehicle modification	2.2	6.6

had a total of 1,763 claims honored, for an average of 43 per family (range 2-190).

The families provided us with specific information on 95 unhonored claims. In most of the cases (81%), the families and others felt the rejected service was crucial enough to pursue payment for it from other sources. When funding could not be secured, parents or other family members covered all or part of the cost in 88% of these instances. In 13% of the instances, other sources such as friends, local charities, foundations, or targeted local fund-raising drives contributed to paying for the services. As can be seen from Table 2.14, which summarizes the costs for 46 of the services that were paid for exclusively with private funds, some of these costs were substantial.

The interview data make it clear that even with extensive insurance coverage, many families experienced major additional household expenditures. Examples of these expenditures follow.

> Ramp on house at the front door for wheelchair. Wheelchair, special helmet, braces, eye glasses, hearing aids, hospital bed and rail, restraints when violent. (AR01)

> The following are monthly expenses. Right now insurance is paying all. However, in July the insurance will cap out. (1) All equipment and supplies: $3,600—suction catheter, feeding bags, ventilator circuit, tubing (has to be changed every 48 hours). (2) Nurses—allowed through insurance—16 hours/day. (3) O.T.—$560 per month for 8 visits a month at $70. P.T.—

TABLE 2.14
Range of Disability Related Expenses Covered by Private Sources

COST OF SERVICE ($)	n
1–19	2
20–99	8
100–199	0
200–499	6
500–999	8
1000–1,999	8
2000–4,999	4
5000–9,999	6
10,000–29,999	2
30,000–50,000	1
>50,000	1
Total	46

$480 per month for 8 visits a month at $60. (4) Overall cost and care of hospitalizations and procedures and treatment while in hospital: $475,000. (5) Parents now owe $5,000. This is balance from when insurance paid 80% of cost. (6) Out-of-pocket expense per month: (a) balance at hospital (#5 above): $50. (b) medication (Ventolin for breathing—2 bottles every 1½ weeks): $70. (c) ranitidine (4-month supply): $100. (d) distilled water for digestive track: 5 gallons per week. (FL03)

We had to find another place to live with first floor bedroom, widened doorways, enlarged front porch, central air, ramp, van, washer and dryer. House renovations: $10,000. Van: $18,500. Air: $1,450. Porch: $1,400. Ramp: $1,000. Washer and dryer: $1,100. Furnishings to accommodate supplies: $800. Generator for emergency power. We've got the following equipment: Suction machine, portable suction machine, hospital bed, air pressure mattress, wheelchair, room monitor, humidifier, bath chair, oxygen, air cleaner, gastrostomy tube pump, breathing treatment machine. And all the following expenses have gone up: formula, diapers, appliances, utility bills, medications. (MI07)

Another factor contributing to the cost of providing care is time off from work for Individual Education Plan meetings or to respond to crises. During the year before the interview, 83.7% of the people we interviewed had to take some time off from work because of the care needs of the child; 49% of this group had to take time off at least once a month. Additionally, 75% indicated that a spouse or other adult in the home had to take time off from work, and almost a third of this group (32%) needed to take time off at least once a month.

A major problem that many families encounter is lack of complete information about what their insurance will cover and what the appropriate procedures are to assure reimbursement.

> Mom was picking up meds at blood bank. In the past she had picked up meds through the hospital, and they had billed insurance. She assumed the blood bank would file the same way and insurance would be billed. However, 6 months after this pick-up, Marsha was billed the cost of Factor 8 ($1,000/6 bottles—family uses 4 times that each year). She called the hospital and they reported that her claim was denied because she had failed to file the expense as "major medical." Now picks up Factor 8 at the Health Department where the appropriate forms are filed. She pays off the other bill a little at a time. (VA07)

A universal issue appears to be the drawn out process of payment to home care providers. Many families in the study group told of the trouble they had obtaining or retaining services simply because providers must wait so long to be paid.

> We were supposed to be covered since January 1—real difficult—not paying bills. Nothing has gone through—no one has been paying for bills. Currently owe $25,000 to the provider for home health care. The whole insurance situation is a complicated mess. The bottom line is that there are over $25,000 in medical bills and lots of uncertainty. I don't know if or when bills will be paid by insurance companies. There's lots of confusion about what is and what isn't covered. (MN07)

When slow payment and lack of information are further complicated by the bureaucratic that confronts these families, parents can find themselves without services even when they have done everything they are supposed to.

> There were problems with Medicaid. He qualified for care at home at State level, but local level refused to qualify him. State had to demand that it be processed. He was thrown out of care at home and then picked up by regular Medicaid. He was then disqualified from the Medicaid because of income. The State is now actively trying to get him reinstated. (NY17)

In an effort to avoid these problems, some of the families take the path of least resistance. Many parents, however, cannot afford to take this approach.

> To fight with insurance company is more trouble than it's worth. No claims need to be filed now. At one point spending over $100 a month on enzymes. (MN03)

Some of these families have been forced to the end of their fiscal ropes and, in order to survive, have developed expertise in "gaming" the system.

The doctors have refused services because she has Medicaid. Had to trick doctors to get the services and then tell the doctor that she had Medicaid. Otherwise they wouldn't help her. (NY18)

Indeed it is surprising that these parents are not more cynical, particularly in their dealings with the Medicaid system, which, according to anecdotal reports, is capricious and governed by seemingly irrational regulation.

She used to purchase suction catheters from a provider in Richmond, VA, to save money. Now Medicaid says she must purchase them through a Waynesboro, VA, provider even though they cost more—because Medicaid wants to deal with a single provider for the area. (VA03)

One of the most frustrating experiences that these families shared is the lack of responsiveness of professionals and insurers to what the parents feel are the specific needs of their children.

They won't cover a wheelchair—that will lead to larger medical problems later on. Can't get correctional shoes. Can't get things to make Suzie's life easier and more functional that we can't afford. Can't buy better bed to help her sleep; needs wheelchair. Suzie was sleeping on waterbed which helped but had to sell. Can't buy adaptive toys (for example, one toy costs $39.95). Can't buy standing board, side-line chair, corner chair. (AR09)

Some families reported that they had been targeted for loss of benefits after their costs exceeded some apparently predetermined ceiling of acceptable risk.

Insurance coverage for this family in the state of Florida has been almost impossible. Turned down for assistance even from Children's Medical Services at the local teaching hospital. Right now they are being forced out of the spouse's work group insurance because of the conditions of both children. The mother states that the insurance makes it clear that it's because of them, e.g., their premiums as of June 18, 1989, will go up $608 per month—and that's the father's share. Her husband brings home $1,000 per month. After paying their insurance they would have no money for food and house payments. The father is now looking at other job possibilities. Consequently, depending on type of job and where vacancies are, they could very well have to move and they would have to because they need the insurance coverage—so whatever it takes

In some cases, the doctors have just written off their claims because they were aware of the burden. One insurance company they dealt with in 1985 cancelled them after 3 months. They were without insurance for 9 months. At one point there was a $120,000 total when the parents were uninsured and had to try to pay out of pocket. She states that they had to liquidate assets, sell all their stock, and cash in their life insurance policies in order to pay some of this. (FL11)

Getting What My Child Needs

The survey asked families to reflect on their experiences in securing the various services that impinge on the lives of their child and family, and we tried to differentiate services intended to meet the care needs of the child from those that supported the family. For the most part, this distinction worked quite well. The exceptions were those services that were identified as service coordination, discharge planning, or case management. In the discussion which follows, we attempt to distinguish those case coordination efforts that focused almost exclusively on obtaining services for the child from those which focused on the child within the context of the family.

Table 2.15 presents the range of services received by the children in the study group. Most of the children were receiving services from multiple providers and multiple systems. In fact, 51% of the children received services from 4 or more providers. It is instructive and a bit disconcerting that although they were at the center of very complex service networks, only 18.6% of the families received case management or service coordination services. In general, the families were satisfied with the services their children did receive: 74.6% of families rated them as satisfactory or excellent, while 25.4% rated services as less than satisfactory. The families were even more enthusiastic in endorsing the value of the child centered services: 87.8% rated them as valuable.

Many of the families related stories of very positive interactions with individual therapists and physicians who have known them and their children for a long time and have acted as major sources of support and advocates within the system. Families reported that these professionals developed a real responsiveness to the unique characteristics of the families and attempted to provide truly individualized, family-centered services.

Unfortunately, these positive feelings are balanced by many stories of "detached" professional behavior or, worse, professional providers who, at least in the parents' minds, came across as callous.

> Mary was in school and started to complain to the teacher of her throat hurting and she wanted to call her mother. She was prevented from doing so. By the time she got home in the afternoon she had gotten progressively worse and the mother had to take her in to the doctor immediately. Needless to say, the mother was very put out with school. She stated that she told the teacher not to ever do it again. It's typical in the sense of the fact the diabetic condition makes Mary highly sensitive to anything, so all conditions and circumstances have to be investigated and monitored. What

TABLE 2.15
Services Received by Children with Specialized Needs in Study Group

SERVICE	% RECEIVING SERVICE
School	66.4
Physical therapy	41.3
Outpatient medical	20.5
Case management	18.6
Camp	17.4
Home nursing	15.3
Dental care	15.2
Inpatient medical	13.1
Other	12.1
After school program	12.1
Speech therapy	12.0
Home health aide	12.0
Occupational therapy	11.9
Transportation	11.0
Adaptive equipment	9.9
Counseling	9.8
Respiratory therapy	8.7
Vision care	8.7
Other specialized therapy	7.7
Recreation activity	7.6
Discharge planning	6.6
Equipment maintenance	5.5
Behavioral therapy	5.5
Vocational/pre-vocational	4.4
Home adaptations	2.2
Life support equipment	1.1
Adult day program	1.1

was unusual was the fact that the teacher didn't contact the mother. The teacher thought Mary was "faking." The mother's contention was that even so because of Mary's diabetes (of which she had previously explained to teacher), Mary has to be monitored, and the mother should have been called. (FL06)

Many parents also recount incidents in which professionals ignored their input and insight into the child's condition:

Mother has had to fight for the IEP goals. She has been battling the district for a long time. Now he receives 45 minutes/week of in-home contact with a social worker. She sees the school personnel as largely inept and not able to provide him with services he needs. Mother has had a difficult time convincing the schools of the neurological basis of his difficulties. He was even once put into an experimental school for an "open education" program which was too chaotic and pressured—exactly the kind of environment that makes him confused and act up. Homework was never done. He was being chained to his desk by 6th grade. He began running off. He was punished at the district level.

Mother complained also that the school wanted to control his whole life: church, friends, and she resented this. The attendance review board went into their private habits.

Although Franco had not passed school requirements, he was sent to junior high school because they didn't know what else to do with him. He failed 2 years. More punishment. Once he rang a fire bell on a dare and was given total suspension for 3 weeks. There was no instruction during this time and Franco was falling hopelessly behind. Because of dazed look he has been accused of being on drugs. (CA10)

Some parents react to professional indifference with understandable concern and suspicion:

Mom told several nightmare stories about encountering physicians who didn't understand enough about how cerebral palsy affects a person's tone and motor capability to make appropriate diagnosis of Allen.

On one occasion, Allen complained of a pain in his side. She noted other symptoms and rushed him into emergency. This was early one morning. The doctors were unable to diagnose the problem. Fortunately, around seven that evening Allen's pediatrician came by the hospital (for some reason the other doctors had not contacted him) to see another patient. Mom nabbed him to look at Allen. After a brief exam he diagnosed a ruptured appendix. Luckily, Allen recovered. (VA04)

George's school experience hints that such contradictory behavior on the part of professionals demonstrates that they are more in tune with some of the misperceptions held by the uninformed general public than they are with the state of the art in best practice regarding services to children with specialized needs.

George's teacher once gave his class a lecture on muscular dystrophy, saying to a full class how George would be dead by age 20. He felt bad for other peers but is full of hope and inspiration for others. Mom has fought all types of battles. The most receptive was the principal of the local elementary school, who made all the necessary accommodations, but once George hit special ed things became complex and went down hill. (NY13)

The high ratings that parents gave to the services they received seem to contradict the qualitative interview data that reflect problematic experiences with specific professionals. There are two possible explanations for

TABLE 2.16

Family Support Services Received

SERVICE	% RECEIVING SERVICE
Parent network	31.5
Respite	23.6
Newsletter	22.9
Advocacy group	21.7
Other	14.1
Parent instruction	13.1
Service coordination	13.0
Counseling	12.0
Financial assistance	10.9
Parent advocacy/training	8.7
Information	8.7
Transportation	5.5
Future financial planning	3.3
Day care	2.2
Adaptive design consultation	2.2
Homemaker	1.1

this dichotomy. First, most of these parents have had few or no services and so were grateful for what they do receive. Second, the difficulties described in the narratives center around efforts to secure and maintain services and do not relate to the quality of the services.

Mom told the interviewer, "You know, I am so tired of being a pioneer. I fought for accessible school busses, we got George into the accelerated classrooms, we were in court for the first five years [after diagnosis] more than we were at home. I just want to follow for now because my son is failing and I want this time to be special and uncomplicated." Mom feels that George will need nursing eventually and that will really be a lot of traffic in the home—so she wants quiet and calm time. (NY13)

Family Supports

Table 2.16 summarizes the range of services that fall under the broad umbrella of "family supports" rather than clinical services for the child with special needs. When these services are compared with the range of supports listed as the components of a comprehensive system of family supports (see chapter 3), one is impressed by the very limited array of support services actually secured by these families. This fact is further underscored by the fact that 41% of the services reported by the study group resulted from membership in traditional parent advocacy organizations such as the Association for Retarded Citizens, the Autism Society, and so forth (i.e., parent network, newsletter, advocacy group). As in the case of child-centered services, the families highly valued the supports they received: 80% were satisfied with what they received.

When we turn to the information obtained through the interviews, the limitations on true "family support" become clearer. The responses to inquiries in this area highlight both the need for specific support services and the unproductive interactions that many of these families have had with professionals and agency "gatekeepers."

> When Malcolm was released from the hospital the family was patted on the back and told that they could always "bring him back." That was the discharge plan. Melissa was a nurse's aide and was involved all along with Malcolm's care, but they were not very well trained. (NY07)

The inadequacy of traditional professional preparation is underscored by the frequency with which families encountered providers, administrators, and others who were completely out-of-touch with the idea of community-based, family-centered care.

> As Colin got worse, both parents ended up unemployed. DSHS commented, "White middle class folks looking for something for nothing." Because initial reports were that Colin would only live 2 years, they have been refused. Governor's aide recommended getting a divorce so could help through state. (WA04)

Often the root of the problem can be traced to the complete lack of ongoing communication and coordination.

> Mom has been asking for help since Mario's birth. She is tired. She finds out about programs and goes for them. She is really her own best advocate. She will be inexhaustible where Mario is concerned. "You are a parent that should have no problems because you know so much and are so strong." That is what a social worker told her. Mom says, "I would rather see a little action than hear that nonsense."

> Mom is so strong she even told the Department of Social Services in her county when they did the application over 4 months ago for the "waiver" (still no waiver to date) that if they documented all the necessary services via her MDs "wasn't the county committing child abuse to not put those services in?" They did not respond. She even had her husband call the county to say that she was "cracking up and needed help." Their response was, "We can put him on the waiting list, which extends over two years for out-of-home placement." She is furious and says, "I can't even go crazy because they just simply do not care."

> The same people in this small rural county who are doing the waiver forms have known Mario since birth and are now asking for all the medical care

TABLE 2.17
Forms of Public Support Desired by Study Group

TYPE OF SUPPORT	% INDICATING DESIRABLE
True flexibility in all aspects of services to families	23
Responsive family-focused professionals (especially service brokers)	21
Development of positive attitudes toward people with disabilities and special health care needs	21
Financial assistance	20
Readily available information and referral	19
Accessibility/integration of community services	15
Reform of health care and health insurance	14
Parent support groups	14
Respite and day care	12

history since birth. "The question I have is what have they been doing in my home all these years!" (NY12)

Most families found themselves being asked to master a system that is totally new to them. They found their energies diverted from being a parent to being a case manager. By implication, if parents can master this coordination game then they must be good parents and therefore merit preferential treatment.

As part of our effort to understand what these families defined as family support, we asked them a series of interrelated, open-ended questions about what they needed to make their days go easier, what would contribute to the well-being of their families and children, and how the public sector can best support them. When these responses were examined, a consistent core of supports was identified. These responses are summarized in Table 2.17.

It is noteworthy that many families did not necessarily translate their individual needs into the specific supports they wanted from the public sector. For example, an Arkansas mother said she needed assistance in housework, help with transportation, and some respite; yet the major support she sought from the public sector was access to a "big brother" organization that would provide her son with a friend and integrated recreation opportunities. What surprised us in reviewing this pattern of responses was the degree to which these families seemed to be calling for basic reform of the service system toward greater parent control, responsiveness, and flexibility rather than just expansion of services. On the personal level, most of the families identified specific service needs, but when it came to what they wanted from the public sector, for the most part they identified issues and services that were more systemic in focus.

TABLE 2.18
Projected Uses for Direct Financial Assistance

TYPE OF SERVICE	% OF FAMILIES
Transportation	24
Special equipment and home adaptations	23
Family entertainment/recreation	21
Respite and child care	20
In-home aides, tutors, and therapist	20
Food	19
Clothing	16
Medical and dental	13
Supplies (e.g. diapers, over the counter medication, etc.)	11
Housing	8
Medication	8
Utilities	8
Present or future school costs	4
Saving for future cost of care	3
Health insurance	2

The majority of families who called for direct financial aid to families felt they could exercise greater control over the services for their child by hiring directly.

As one measure of what families identified as their most pressing needs, we asked them to tell us how they would spend $250 a month if they were to receive it in the form of direct financial assistance. For some of the families in Michigan, Minnesota, and Arkansas, states that had either established or were field-testing a direct cash assistance program, this question was not hypothetical, and these families reported on how they were actually spending the money. A summary of family responses is found in Table 2.18.

Because many of the families needed to use special clinics or other services that were not in their neighborhoods, the high ranking given to transportation is not surprising. In addition, a substantial minority of families felt that their current day-to-day transportation needs were not being adequately addressed. A number of the families indicated that cash assistance would be used to cover the cost of specialized diet and adaptive clothing, but 8–10% of the study group, falling in the lowest income stratum, indicated they would use the aid to meet their basic day-to-day living expenses. On the other extreme, several of the more prosperous families indicated that they would use the money for their child's long-term security and would establish trust accounts for future schooling or adult service needs.

The high ranking for family entertainment/recreation can be explained in two ways. For some families, extra money would allow them to do some of those things they have had to forego because of the extra cost associated with the child's disability or medical condition. In other words, "We'll use it to do the things that all our neighbors do, but that we haven't been able to afford." The second projected use of cash assistance for entertainment was to provide out-of-home opportunities for the child with a disability through the purchase of equipment, transportation, aides, or memberships or registration fees.

The Daily Battles

Though families face consistent challenges, most parents do not see the demands of care as a "burden" but as part of being a loving parent. What they consistently identify as their major burdens and sources of stress are (a) the continual struggles they must go through to get the supports they need to appropriately care for their child; and (b) professional attitudes that seem to discount the central role of *home* and *parenting* in the lives of children with disabilities and special health care needs. This is reflected in the high preference families gave to flexibility, responsive professional, information, and positive attitudes as major supports for families. Families interviewed want the system to change so that they no longer have to battle to receive services—battles that in some cases, have been waged for years. As Jim's mother put it:

> *Mom:* "I do not understand why they fight us tooth and nail for every little thing and would not ask us a single question if we left and abandoned him to an institution. Our newest battle is now the school system. We are now in court at great expense to our family so that Jim can get the nursing he needs at school. I am a little tired of being a pioneer. We are fighting like this to get him into BOCES—can you imagine what it is going to be like to get him into elementary school?"
>
> Dad sits on a lot of statewide coalitions and even with his visibility things are a struggle. Both parents are tired and would love to go back to just being a family. (NY11)

Another consistent finding is the frustration and, in many cases, anger the families feel over the incredible lengths to which they must go to get even minimal support and assistance for their child. It is disturbing to hear parents speak of the arbitrary manner in which the state, health care providers, local education authorities, insurance companies, and home care providers dealt with them. Again and again families reported being treated as if they were trying to defraud the system rather than attempting to secure services to which they were entitled.

> When are they going to realize that people shouldn't be forced to live at poverty level in order to receive assistance. Could have benefits if you do dumb things—get divorced, quit job, etc. For example, my husband was told by some bureaucrat that he was being an "irresponsible father" by having a job that is paid on commission. Penalized for being good parents, staying home with the children. How can we raise strong, healthy individuals without parents around? To get financial assistance is worse than going to a bank to ask for a loan—it's more degrading—we "make too much money—not in debt bad enough"—WHAT?! When we apply for help, we need to reinvent the wheel—need 50 copies of income tax—forms, forms, forms—then maybe they'll talk to you. (MN03)

George's parents have had years of experience in dealing with the system and were quite articulate regarding the basic issues that younger families were only beginning to confront. As his mother put it:

> It isn't the child or young person that makes you crazy—it is the system. I also don't understand why the social workers at the hospital for the past 17 years have not connected us to some kind of supports . . . The PHCP paperwork for billing had to be completed and sent back to PHCP by the social worker at the University clinic to start payment for the home health care agency, this process was so delayed that we almost lost their services.

His father said:

> I don't understand why it is necessary to call on outside advocates to intervene to get these issues resolved. Why are our services always dependent on the good will of a particular social worker when the family assumes they are doing their job? Why do you have to monitor people who are supposed to be helping you? (NY13)

Even when a family thinks that all of the problems have been worked out in advance, they often learn they are confronting a constant series of battles to maintain the supports they thought were all arranged.

> The regular O.T. person was out on maternity leave and had been out since October. The mother had not been able to receive another therapist because the next available person couldn't make home visits. (FL01)

This lack of consistency and the apparently arbitrary actions of multiple public and private professionals intensify the families' feelings of alienation and tension, adding to the natural anxiety that they have about their child's condition. They must deal with the ever present fear that someone will do something to topple their carefully constructed support systems, which they all realize are fragile. This tension effectively subverts one of the basic principles of family supports: to enable the family to be a family and the parents to devote their principal energies to parenting.

I'm really afraid the system may not respond to meet needs before she dies from her illness. Hours doing battle are hours spent not nurturing. (WA06)

Mary's mother confirms that many family support programs operate on the squeaky wheel principle. In other words, if parents are vocal, well informed, or politically well connected, then eventually they will get some response.

At one point before receiving financial assistance, mother was working three jobs and trying to take care of a sick baby, and couldn't do it all. She then had to let it go and begin applying for some financial assistance until she could do better. She also was fired from a job because she left because Helen was having an insulin reaction.

She was treated like she was nothing. She felt very frustrated by the "system." She was told she didn't qualify because of living with her sister and she explained her circumstances, i.e., single parent, low income, and she didn't eat or cook with her sister. She then said to the worker, "Something is wrong with this system, and I want to talk with someone else." She was told, "Don't get nasty." She stated that all of this made her feel like she wasn't a good person. She then persisted and after several visits was able to see someone else who said she did qualify. She also now qualifies for AFDC and receives $220 per month and $105 per month in food stamps. She is now enrolled in a nursing program with completion hopefully next year and says she is now looking for part-time employment. (FL06)

The other side of the squeaky wheel principle is that some families do not get services to which they are entitled because they do not have the knowledge, strength, or connections to endure. Further, because obtaining these services is essentially an adversarial process, even the "empowered" family finds it a taxing experience.

The Future

The future is a difficult issue for many of these families. The major traumas they have endured thus far, the constant battle to obtain support services, the financial strains, the re-ordering of their social world, and most of all, the day-after-day care needs of their children have led them to adopt a perspective which takes life one day at a time.

She wants to do everything she can and is asked to do by physicians to insure that Tim is aided to his fullest potential. She states that she tries not to make long-term plans. She wants to take one day at a time. Always looking for what Tim can do because of his own spirit.

She has been told that Tim will probably develop asthma, some aspects of cerebral palsy, will probably be hospitalized five times by age 9–10 years, and will have a low tolerance to respiratory illness. If he doesn't grow he could also develop emphysema. All of the above are her concerns, but again she says she is going to take one day at a time. (FL01)

This "live for today" attitude, which was consistently reported throughout the interviews, is further reinforced by the big question marks regarding the future. The parents of children with degenerative or terminal conditions consciously chose not to dwell on the future but rather to devote their physical and psychological energies to making the most of the present moment. Families of children who need lifelong supports also shared this attitude. In these cases, it is possible that not thinking about the future is one way that parents can conserve their energies for the battles yet to be fought.

The question of the future led Pete's mother to note that her son's future depends on fundamental changes not in the system of services but in our society's basic attitudes toward people with significant disabilities. Specifically, she referred to the artificial limits that our culture places on the ability of people with disabilities to achieve their full potential.

> I can't bear to think about the future (if Pete was not disabled his prospects would be wonderful). Pete is a great kid, he works hard and is talented as an artist, and academically. His aspirations are tremendous, he will undoubtedly have much to contribute to society, if he ever gets the chance. Realistically I doubt that Pete will get the chance in our present society. If he does what will it cost him in lost Medicaid coverage? Will he be able to pursue a career?
>
> One of my chief sources of stress is what will happen to Pete when I am gone. If money or property is left to Pete he will probably lose Medicaid coverage. Then what? Who will advocate for him and protect him? Who will assure that he is cared for? Is this bright, funny, loving little boy doomed to live on welfare? Or will he choose not to continue living at all when he finally realizes that his hard work and achievements are all for naught? I hope that by the time Pete reaches adulthood, our society will provide him with other choices, like being a contributing functioning member of the community who can use his skills to remain self sufficient without losing medical services and care he needs.
>
> It is traditional in our country for parents to work hard in an effort to help their children attain a better position in life. Most parents promote the best opportunities for growth and learning in an effort to help their children develop. When parents die their children are usually left with the benefits of parents' hard work. Why is a disabled child not entitled to this? Why must he choose between the health care he needs to survive and a decent

home to live in or the self-esteem that comes from self-sufficiency and earning a living at a challenging job which allows him to use his exceptional talents? (NY15)

SUMMARY AND CONCLUSIONS

This chapter examined the experiences of families of children with a variety of specialized needs, families who, as pioneers in family-centered, community-based care, are defining the future of services. It also looked at the services that are supposed to support the families in their efforts. On one hand, we have exposed the reader to the tension between traditional approaches to services for children with special needs and the expressed needs of families for coherence and empowerment. On the other hand, the data testify to the development of a new definition of the parent-professional relationship as individual professionals and select service systems around the country strive to work out what it means to support families.

When the testimony of these families is carefully read, we are left with an impression of a schizophrenic system of public and private supports for home care for children with severe disabilities and specialized health care needs. The official rhetoric affirms the primacy of the family, and yet the experience of these families is otherwise. Again and again, the families told of benefits managers, case managers, discharge planners, social workers, program administrators, special educators, and the like who implied that parents were out to "milk the system." This attitude was conveyed even in dealing with entitlements and plans to which the parents had long contributed. Families were treated as beneficiaries of benevolent charity for which they should be grateful. Families, already struggling to come to terms with their child's impairment and the care demands assocated with it, find themselves stigmatized, impoverished, and degraded. In a society of rugged individualists they are forced to ask for help. That in itself is more than some of the parents can deal with.

It should be clear that these parents are not asking for charity. No one here is out to "milk the system." They are simply seeking support to meet some of the extraordinary demands associated with raising their children. As parents, they are not looking for the state to assume their responsibilities. Rather, they seek supports that will enable them to devote their energies to being parents. Their testimony suggests the need for states to recognize support for the family as an entitlement that affirms that the family.

They base this call on the fact that support for families is the most cost effective service the state can provide. By supporting families and aiding the integration of children with disabilities and special health care needs in their home communities and neighborhood schools, the state will shape the future demand for adult services in a manner that places much greater reliance on the already existing resources of our communities and less on expensive specialized service settings.

REFERENCES

Agosta, J. M. (1989). Using cash assistance to support family efforts. In L. K. Irvin & G. H. S. Singer (Eds.), *Support for caregiving families: Enabling positive adaptation to disability*. Baltimore: Brookes.

Ashbaugh, J., Spence, R., Lubin, R., Houlihan, J., & Langer, M. (1985). *Summary of data on handicapped children and youth*. Cambridge, MA: Human Services Research Institute.

Bogdan, R., & Biklen, S. (1983). *Qualitative research for education: Introduction to theory and methods*. Boston, MA: Allyn and Bacon.

Herman, S. E. (1983). *Family support services: Reports on meta-evaluation studies*. Lansing, MI: Michigan Department of Mental Health.

Karnes, M. B., & Teska, J. A. (1980). Towards successful parent involvement in programs for handicapped children. In J. J. Gallagher (Ed.), *New directions for exceptional children: Parents and families of handicapped children*. San Francisco: Jossey-Bass.

Koop, C. E. (1987). *Surgeon General's report: Children with special health care needs*. Rockville, MD: U.S. Department of Health and Human Services, Public Health Service.

Maternal and Child Health. (1988). *Family-centered care*. Rockville, MD: U.S. Department of Health and Human Services, Public Health Services.

Minnesota Developmental Disabilities Program. (1983). *The Minnesota family subsidy program: Its effects on families with a developmentally disabled child* (Policy Analysis No. 18). St. Paul: Minnesota Developmental Disabilities Planning Council.

Moore, J. A., Hamerlynck, L. A., Barsh, E. T., Spieker, S., & Jones, R. (1982). *Extending family resources* (2nd ed.). Seattle: University of Washington, Children's Clinic and Preschool.

Nelkin, V. (1987). *Family-centered health care for medically fragile children: Principles and practices*. Washington, DC: Georgetown University, Child Development Center.

Parrott, M. E., & Herman, S. E. (1987). *Report on the Michigan family support subsidy program*. Lansing: Michigan Department of Mental Health.

Rosenau, N. (1983). *Final evaluation of a family support program*. Macomb-Oakland, MI: Macomb County Community Mental Health and Macomb-Oakland Regional Center.

Snell, M. E., & Beckman-Brindley, S. (1984). Family involvement in intervention with children having severe handicaps. *Journal of the Association for the Severely Handicapped, 9*, 213–230.

Stabenow, D. (1983). *The family support subsidy act: Questions and answers on P.A. 249 of 1983* (H.B. 4448). Lansing, MI: State Capitol, 412 Roosevelt Building.

Zimmerman, S. (1984). The mental retardation family subsidy program: Its effects on families with a mentally handicapped child. *Family Relations, 33*, 105–118.

Chapter 3

Supporting Families
State Family Support Efforts

James Knoll
Susan Covert
Ruth Osuch
Susan O'Connor
John Agosta
and
Bruce Blaney

INTRODUCTION

The 1980s saw the broad family agenda gain some degree of attention in state and national policy deliberations. As the decade progressed, issues surrounding day care and parental leave appeared with increasing frequency in the daily press and on the evening news. As family concerns in general gained prominence, the special concerns and needs of families of people with disabilities emerged as central issues in the debate over this nation's policy regarding people with disabilities. If events in the 1980s have helped to define the agenda, the policies of the 1990s will determine whether the agenda is translated into concrete supports and expanded services.

Central to this changing awareness have been efforts to re-examine and redefine the relationship between the public sector and families of children and adults with disabilities and between such families and formal helping networks. One of the earliest critics of the emerging pattern of "community-based" services was Skarnulis (1979), who called for policy makers and providers to stop "supplanting" the family and start supporting it. The wisdom of this observation, although not lost on some administrators and providers concerned with family support, has taken a decade to influence the national trends in the field.

The "support not supplant" philosophy coupled with changes in the political and economic climate ushered in a period of unparalleled interest

---

Acknowledgment. Preparation of this chapter was supported with funds from the Administration on Developmental Disabilities, Office of Human Development Services, U.S. Department of Health and Human Services, under grant number 90DD0156. All opinions expressed herein are solely those of the authors and do not reflect the position or policy of the Department of Health and Human Services.

57

in the development of services for people with disabilities within the family home. On the federal level, the terms "family support," "family-centered," and "community-based" pervaded the requests for proposals and conference agendas of almost every relevant agency (Administration on Developmental Disabilities, 1988; Koop, 1987; Nelkin, 1987; Shaffer & Cross, 1989). This was accompanied by the development of a variety of new federal programmatic initiatives, most notably waivers and other Medicaid options, which were designed specifically to provide for services to people with disabilities in the family. As previous research in the field and the findings of this report clearly demonstrate, these developments on the national stage have been at least equalled at the state and local level:

- Researchers have begun to shift their focus from a concentration on disability as a source of stress within the family to an increased emphasis on the impact of various support strategies on families (see for examples Dunst, Trivette, & Deal, 1988; Gallagher & Vietze, 1986; Knoll & Bedford, 1989; Singer & Irvin, 1989).
- A series of publications appeared over the decade that tracked the gradual development of family support policy and outlined the options available to policy makers (Agosta & Bradley, 1985; Bates, 1985; Bird, 1984; Braddock, Hemp, Fujiura, Bachelder, & Mitchell, 1990; Cohen, Agosta, Cohen, & Warren, 1989; Taylor, Lakin, & Hill, 1989).
- During the 1980s, there were several efforts to make the intricacies of financing family support and home care accessible to parents and providers (e.g., Ellison, Bradley, Knoll, & Moore, 1989; Gaylord & Leonard, 1988)
- A number of publications provided parents with readily accessible information to aid them in supervising services within the home (Goldfarb, Botherson, Summers, & Turnbull, 1986; Jones, 1985; Kaufman & Lichtenstein, 1986).
- Guides were published to assist parents in actually influencing the development of services in their community (Bronheim, Cohen, & Magrab, 1985; Hazel et al., 1988).
- A final distinct group of publications synthesized the developing trends in family support and identified the values or principles that should guide public policy towards people with disabilities and their families. Most of these efforts were intended to provide advocates with a clear agenda to organize efforts at systems change (e.g., United Cerebral Palsy Associations, 1987). Some reports emerged as parts of federally sponsored projects aimed at the needs of children with severe disabilities (Center on Human Policy, 1987) and with special health care needs (Maternal and Child Health, 1988).

This growing literature underscores the expanding interest in family support. However, the reality is that few families in this country have yet to experience anything like the ideal of family support articulated in chapter 1. Though each new fiscal year brings substantial growth in family support programs around the country, other programs lapse because they were pilot projects that did not become permanent. Further, many family support initiatives are not firmly established by legislative mandate and therefore are susceptible to the vicissitudes of the state budgetary process. These factors underscore the often tentative and embryonic nature of family support efforts in the United States and the need for current information regarding the status of family support activities.

The compartmentalization of family support and the lack of interagency collaboration have constrained efforts to develop a comprehensive overview of state commitments to family support. Families of children with a developmental disability may technically be eligible for assistance from some or all of the following agencies in their state: health, maternal and child health, Title V, social service, mental health, retardation, child protection, education, early intervention, pilot projects funded by the state developmental disabilities council, and others. These agencies may have complementary or even potentially duplicative programs. Unfortunately, no state has taken a comprehensive interagency approach to family support in an effort to maximize access to these resources. As a result, knowledge about services is often limited to people working in a discrete program.

This chapter describes a national survey of family support activities and provides a basic core of information regarding the status of family support at the beginning of the 1990s. Though it is primarily focused on developmental disabilities programs, it does provide a baseline for continuing surveys.

METHODS

The study reported in this chapter was designed as one aspect of a larger effort to provide states with technical assistance related to the development of a systematic approach to family supports. Discussions with policy makers, providers, and parent groups around the country and a review of the literature crystallized the need to develop an up-to-date base of information on the current status of state family support efforts before launching into an intensive technical assistance effort.

In an effort to address these limitations, a data collection instrument was designed to gain a thorough description of the full range of efforts in family support in each state. The data collection strategy was a phone interview and a "snowballing" approach to sampling in which each informant was asked to nominate other knowledgeable persons to be interviewed. Using this approach, data were collected until either no new subjects were identified or no new information was obtained.

The point of entry into each state was the state Developmental Disabilities Planning Council. A letter was sent to the executive director of each council explaining our effort and asking for an appointment for a phone interview or direction to another person in the state who could provide us with an overview of family supports. A second letter was sent to any council that did not reply. If no response was received to this second inquiry, a phone call was made to set up an appointment or identify an alternate informant. As a result of this process, interviews were scheduled for all 50 states (we were unsuccessful in securing a contact in the District of Columbia).

A field test of the interview guide was conducted, and the interview protocol was revised and shortened. The revised protocol asked the informants to describe the major aspects of their state's family support efforts. The instrument consists of 46 items in the following categories: general background, funding level, number of families served, eligibility criteria, administrative practices, programmatic practices, level of family control, implementation problems, program effectiveness, informant's evaluation of the program, related efforts in the state, efforts at service coordination, state Medicaid policy, interagency collaboration, generic services/informal supports, future directions, lessons learned thus far, and suggested contact persons for further information about family support efforts. The interviews ranged in length from one-half to four hours and averaged about one and one half hours.

The first interview was conducted during the summer of 1989. In most states, a second call was made to the initial informant, and in 33 states, the first interview was followed with an additional interview with some other person associated with services in the state who was able to fill in any gaps remaining after the first interview. A total of 83 individuals were interviewed to collect the information for this study. A draft synopsis of each state's family support practices was sent to the respective informants to review for accuracy in September of 1989. Revisions to the analysis were finalized in December 1989.

The 50 state descriptions were analyzed to identify major implementation issues, which are outlined in the following sections. While we were unable to achieve our original, ambitious goal of developing a comprehensive overview of *all* support efforts targeted to families of children with disabilities in the United States, we are able to report here on all such efforts that are provided through state departments of mental retardation or developmental disabilities or under state developmental disabilities councils. In addition, we have identified many efforts of other state departments on behalf of groups of children with other disabilities and their families. In this regard, the report provides a firm foundation for future efforts to compile a comprehensive guide to all family support activities.

RESULTS

Forty-one states had developed programs with a specific focus on supporting families that are raising a child who has a developmental disability. These programs had provided some service to at least 129,777 families during the state fiscal year that preceded the survey. An overview of these activities is found in Table 3.1. Many of these programs also provided supports for adults with a developmental disability in families. Given the history of limited services to families that raise their child with a disability at home and the distinct issues, such as personal autonomy, that differentiate services for adults from children's services, we chose to concentrate on those aspects of state policy and practice that relate to children.

Spokespersons for the nine states that do not have specific family support programs all contended that they provide in-home services and support to families through their typical community services, early intervention programs, or Medicaid waiver. However, when these programs were reviewed in light of the basic components and approach described in this report, they did not approach the efforts found in many other states. Therefore, in Table 3.1 and in most of the subsequent reporting in this section, we show Kansas, Kentucky, Mississippi, Missouri, New Jersey, North Carolina, Oklahoma, South Dakota, and West Virginia without a designated family support activity. In the state profiles, however, the activities enumerated by the informants in these states as family support are outlined.

Type of Program

There is wide diversity in the extent to which family supports are firmly established in each state (see Table 3.2 for a summary of this information). At the time of the survey only three states (Michigan, Wisconsin, and Minnesota) had relatively comprehensive family supports established by state legislation, and in Minnesota and Wisconsin this legislation is not fully implemented in all counties. Three additional states (New Hampshire, Louisiana, and Illinois) had new legislation which, when fully implemented, would bring them close to a comprehensive array of supports. An additional 14 states had some supports that were mandated by state family support legislation. Since the survey, Colorado, West Virginia, and Oregon have also passed broad-based statutes.

In 18 states, family supports were governed by the policy of the state department responsible for services to people with developmental disa-

TABLE 3.1
Summary of State Family Support Activities

STATE	NATURE OF SUPPORTS	TYPE OF PROGRAM	ELIGIBILITY CRITERIA	LIMITATIONS ON BENEFITS	ALLOWABLE SERVICES	FAMILIES SERVED	FUNDING FY1988–89 ($)
AL	Respite	Pilot	Developmental disability	10 days Some service fees	Respite	65 in-home 378 at camp	325,000
AK	Services in crisis	Pilot	Developmental disability	None established Some services fees	Respite, training, attendant care	436 (30 in special crisis program)	718,000
AZ	1. Financial aid	Budgeted	Developmental disability	$4,800/year with co-pay	Homemaker, home health aid, personal care, shelter assistance, transportation, chores, training, adaptations, repairs, renovations, nurse, equipment	177	Exact funding level unavailable
	2. Respite	Budgeted	Developmental disability	Required co-pay	Respite	2,153	1,500,000
AR	Financial aid	Pilot	Child under 18, needs support to participate in community, returning from out-of-home or in transition, lives in pilot areas	$5,000/year	Respite, special equipment, clothing, environmental modifications, communication aids, ramps/lifts, other items not available or covered by other sources	36	400,000
CA	Services	Mandated	Developmental disability, under 18 years of age		Not limited to special medical, dental, training, homemaker, camp, day care, respite, counseling, behavior modification, equipment, advocacy	25,000	30,511,839
CO	Financial aid	Budgeted	Developmental disability	Family reimbursed up to $3,000/year	Family identifies needs in consultation with regional center worker; very flexible as to allowable costs	115 + 200 get aid from special fund	343,000 + 80,000 to 4 respite projects
CT	1. Respite	Budgeted	Mental retardation or autism		Respite	982	799,472

	2. Respite	Budgeted	Other disabilities	30 days/year	Respite	443	400,000
	3. Financial aid	Budgeted	Child under 18, substantial disability, return from or at risk of institutional placement	$2,000/year	To cover disability-related costs not covered by insurance or others	37	74,000
	4. Financial aid	Pilot	Mental retardation or autism, disability has major impact on home expenses, income <$58,800	$236/month	Cash assistance to be spent at the family's discretion	18	50,000
	5. Financial aid	Pilot	Other disabilities (same as above)	$236/month	(same as above)	18	50,000
DE	Respite	Mandated	Aged, disabled, mentally ill, or physically handicapped	216 hrs/year Family pays up to ⅓ on a sliding scale	Respite	67	75,000
FL	Services	Mandated	Developmental disability	Not specified	Arranged with case manager; have paid for therapies, supplies, equipment, medical, dental, counseling, behavior modification, other costs of care of person with disability	11,336	11,285,234
GA	Combination	Pilot	Mental retardation, income <$30,000	$5,000/year	Day care, counseling, diagnostic, medical, dental, clothing, nutrition, equipment, homemaker, nursing, training, recreation, respite, transportation, other with approval	210	611,562
HI	Financial aid	Budgeted	Developmental disability	$2,000/year reimbursement	Environmental modification, counseling, training, homemaker, transportation, respite, medical, other costs not covered by other source	51	115,000
ID	1. Respite	Budgeted	Substantial disability	18 days/quarter	Respite	182	70,000

continued

TABLE 3.1 Summary of State Family Support Activities *(Continued)*

STATE	NATURE OF SUPPORTS	TYPE OF PROGRAM	ELIGIBILITY CRITERIA	LIMITATIONS ON BENEFITS	ALLOWABLE SERVICES	FAMILIES SERVED	FUNDING FY1988–89 ($)
ID *(cont'd)*	2. Financial aid	Budgeted	Developmental disability, under 21 years of age, eligible for Medicaid, significant parent involvement	$250/month	Diagnostics, equipment, therapies, special diets, medical, dental, home health care, counseling, respite, child care, clothing, transportation, environmental modification, recreation	122	50,000
IL	1. Respite	Budgeted	Developmental disability	180 hrs/year	Respite	3,147	4,400,000
	2. Combination	Pilot	Developmental disability, income <$50,000	$3,000/yr	Case management, cash subsidy, vouchers and reimbursement used to obtain wide range of services and supports as identified by families	200	320,000
IN	Services	Mandated	Developmental disability	$600/year; sliding fee scale	Primarily respite; some traditional services provided on limited basis	600	434,535
IA	Financial aid	Mandated	Severely impaired as per special education classification, under 18 years of age, income <$40,000	$246/month	Subsidy used at family's discretion for expenses related to the special needs of the child with a disability	54	400,000
KS	Services No distinct family support initiatives. Some services to families provided through regional centers	Budgeted	Developmental disability	Individually determined based on need	Case management, respite, preschool, other services	NA	NA
KY	Services No distinct family support initiatives. Some services to families provided through regional centers	Budgeted	Developmental disability	Individually determined based on need Sliding fee scale	Respite and other in-home services as provided through local mental health centers	3,541 services delivered (duplicated count)	Respite: 233,074 Other: 978,720

LA	1. Respite	Budgeted	Physical or mental disability, risk of placement without service	720 hrs/6 mos.	Respite	941	1,270,000
	2. Financial aid	Budgeted	Mental retardation	Individually determined	Reimbursement for needed goods and services–flexible determination	64	334,378
	3. Financial aid	Pilot	Under 18 years of age, severe developmental disability, live in pilot area	$250/month	Individually determined by family	30	200,000
	4. Planning	Mandated			New legislation to plan a comprehensive system of community and family supports		
ME	Respite	Budgeted	Children (<20 years) with special health needs and 1–5 year-olds with mental retardation	24 days/year	Respite	450	1,000,000
	Respite	Budgeted	People with mental retardation or autism age 6–adult		Respite	1,200	500,000
MD	Services	Mandated	Developmental disability, at risk of out-of-home placement		Respite, behavior modification, recreation, equipment, medical supplies, therapies; regarded as payor of last resort	1,500	4,000,000
MA	1. Services	Budgeted	Mental retardation, living with birth/adoptive family	Determined based on individual assessment	Services related to care of family member including transportation, equipment, homemaker, respite, therapies, counseling, others	3,000	3,500,000
	2. Respite	Mandated	Developmental disability	100 hrs/6 mos.	Respite	10,000	15,000,000

continued

TABLE 3.1 Summary of State Family Support Activities (*Continued*)

STATE	NATURE OF SUPPORTS	TYPE OF PROGRAM	ELIGIBILITY CRITERIA	LIMITATIONS ON BENEFITS	ALLOWABLE SERVICES	FAMILIES SERVED	FUNDING FY1988-89 ($)
MI	1. Financial aid	Mandated	Child (<18) with severe disability as defined by special education regulations in birth/adoptive home with income under $60,000	$256/month	Used at family discretion for care of family member with a disability	3,300	9,429,251
	2. Services	Mandated	Developmental disability	Determined based on individual assessment	Case management, respite, training, counseling, support groups, crisis intervention, and others through community mental health center		5,250,000
MN	Financial aid	Mandated	Person with mental retardation or related condition, <22 yrs, eligible for residential placement	$250/month	Grants in amount of costs of services in family service plan including not limited to diagnosis, homemaker, equipment, therapies, transportation, preschool, day care, respite	400 in 46 of 87 counties	1,128,700
MS No distinct family support initiatives. Some services to families provided through the state's pilot early intervention project.							
MO No distinct family support initiatives. Some services to families provided through state's purchase of services	Respite	Mandated	Developmental disability, means test for financial eligibility	21 days/year Other services based on need Sliding fee scale	In addition to respite, early intervention, home health care, and counseling; not all services available in all regions of the state	3,034 duplicated count	3,638,053
MT	1. Services	Budgeted	Developmental disability, child (<18 yrs of age)		Training, equipment, evaluation, therapies, case management, support groups, information and referral	476	1,351,659

MT (cont'd)	2. Financial aid	Budgeted	Developmental disability	$350/year for respite	A cash reimbursement program to help families cover part of the cost of respite	542	284,632
	3. Services	Budgeted	Child (<22 years) with severe disabilities returning home or avoiding out-of-home placement		Including but not limited to case management, medical, respite, day care, home modifications, therapies, homemaker, personal care, advocacy	73	910,912
NE	Financial aid	Mandated	Severe or chronic disability, income below state median and 1. Family of child needing support to stay together, 2. adult needing support to stay employed, or 3. persons needing aid to live independently	$300/month	Home modifications, attendant care, non-medical cost of treatment, counseling, training, home health aide, homemaker, equipment, respite, transportation, others based on individual needs; medical expenses specifically excluded	187	300,000
NV	1. Financial aid	Budgeted	Profound retardation, care at home strains family's resources	$260/month	Use of funds at the discretion of the family, but must describe intended use of funds in application	70	178,478
	2. Respite	Budgeted	Mental retardation, sliding scale based on income (<$30,000)	Based on fee scale	Respite	220	66,000
NH	Services	Mandated	Developmental disability; further criteria in process of development under new family support law	Determined regionally and individually	Case management, respite, early intervention provided as independent services; new law mentions (but does not limit services to) information and referral, respite, home modification, equipment, training, crisis aid, outreach	2,000	3,712,270
NJ Services No distinct family support initiatives. Some services to families provided through state's community services		Budgeted	Developmental disability		Case management, respite, and some assistive devices would be available to people living at home	NA	8,793,000 (estimated)

continued

TABLE 3.1 Summary of State Family Support Activities *(Continued)*

STATE	NATURE OF SUPPORTS	TYPE OF PROGRAM	ELIGIBILITY CRITERIA	LIMITATIONS ON BENEFITS	ALLOWABLE SERVICES	FAMILIES SERVED	FUNDING FY1988–89 ($)
NM	Respite	Budgeted	Developmental disability	Time limited and usually for families in crisis	Respite	NA	187,000
NY	Services	Budgeted	Developmental disability and child (<18 years)	Average benefit $1,000/year	Array of 25 services provided by 450 private programs; core services are respite, transportation, recreation, advocacy, behavior management, financial assistance	24,000	22,500,000
NC	Services — No distinct family support initiatives. Some services to families provided through state's general funding of support services.	Budgeted	Developmental disability	Based on need	A variety of services are offered but the most used is respite	1,700 duplicated count	812,311 + 175,500 for 4 federal respite demonstrations
ND 1. Respite		Budgeted	Developmental disability	180 hrs/year Sliding fee scale	Respite	314	funding below under Services
2. Financial aid		Mandated	Developmental disability, <21 years, financial need	$35/week (reimbursement)	Equipment, therapies, diets, medical/dental, home health care, counseling, respite, clothing, training, child care, recreation, transportation, home modifications, excess cost of health insurance or other cost of care	198	300,000
3. Services		Budgeted	Developmental disability adult or child and financial need	In accord with individual services plan	Respite, case management, skill training, family training, but not equipment or home adaptations	290	3,677,000

OH	Financial aid	Mandated	Developmental disability, income <$78,000 per year, child (<18 years)	$2,500/year Sliding co-pay scale	Voucher or reimbursement for respite, counseling, training, diets, equipment, or home modification	4,646	4,777,305
OK	Services	Budgeted	Mental retardation, Medicaid eligible, over 6 years of age, previously institutionalized or at risk of institutionalization.	NA	Use of Medicaid waiver to provide habilitative services, specialized foster care, assessment, case management	350 people from Hissom class clients	NA

No distinct family support initiative. Some services to families provided through state's Medicaid waiver.

OR	Combination	Pilot	Developmental disability	Flexible, average is $5,000/year	Equipment, clothing, transportation, medical/dental, home health, attendant care, diets, home modifications, respite, training, recreation, counseling	75–85	443,000
PA	Combination	Budgeted	Mental retardation	Individual determination	Respite, therapies, homemaker, financial assistance, home modification, training, recreation, others as needed (availability varies from county to county)	15,000	12,000,000
RI	1. Financial aid	Mandated	Developmental disability, need subsidy to stay at home, 400% federal poverty level	$75/week	As described in individual services plan	91	330,000
	2. Respite	Budgeted	Developmental disability	On sliding fee scale	Respite	400	312,000
	3. Services	Budgeted	Developmental disability, eligible for Medicaid waiver	Individual determination Respite: 90 hrs/6 months	Respite, homemaker, home health aide, assistive devices, case management, home modifications	267	1,225,000

continued

TABLE 3.1 Summary of State Family Support Activities *(Continued)*

STATE	NATURE OF SUPPORTS	TYPE OF PROGRAM	ELIGIBILITY CRITERIA	LIMITATIONS ON BENEFITS	ALLOWABLE SERVICES	FAMILIES SERVED	FUNDING FY1988–89 ($)
SC	Financial aid	Budgeted	Mental retardation or related disability with need for support beyond usual county board services and financial means test	$200/month in 6 mos allotment	Based on individual services plan Respite, case management, training, therapies, evaluation, home modification available through county boards under community services budget	220	220,000
SD	No distinct family support initiatives. Some service to families provided through general funding of developmental services.						
TN	Services	Budgeted	Mental retardation	$3,600/year	Equipment, respite, sitter, nutrition, clothing, adaptation/modification of home/vehicle, child care, other services	59	108,000
TX	1. Financial aid	Mandated	Mental retardation, mental illness, or developmental disability; co-payment if income above state median	$3,600/year, one time $3,600 grant for modifications, required co-pay	Flexible use of voucher/debit card for almost all family requests including health services, counseling, training, respite, attendant care, homemaker, transportation, various household expenses	1,192	4,000,000
	2. Financial aid	Pilot	Developmental disability not served by DMHMR	(same as above)	Use of voucher as above in one pilot county	45–47	315,000
UT	Services	Budgeted	Handicapping condition and need for family supports	Individually determined Average $2,000/year	Respite, homemaker, personal care attendant, some medical, home health, nutrition, therapies, behavior management, training, counseling, others as identified	50–60	447,100

VT	1. Services	Budgeted	Severely emotionally disturbed, <21 years, consideration of special circumstances	Up to 3 mos Average 10 hrs a week in home	Crisis intervention, skill training, counseling, aid in accessing community resources	131	2,000,000
	2. Respite	Budgeted	Severely emotionally disturbed	Being determined	Respite	50–100	200,000
	3. Respite	Budgeted	Mental retardation	264 hrs/yr More time available on sliding fee scale	Families are reimbursed at rate of $3.65 an hour for respite they arrange	400	544,150
VA	Combination	Pilot	Mental retardation or mental illness	$3,600/year	Respite, behavior management, equipment, home modification, others as identified	200	350,000 for 2 years
WA	Services	Mandated	Developmental disability	Authorized on monthly basis	Respite, attendant care, therapies, equipment, home modifications and other adaptations, others as identified and approved	2,500	2,500,000
WV	Services No distinct family support initiatives. Some services to families provided through Community Behavioral Health Centers' services.	Budgeted	Developmental disability	Individually determined	Therapies, respite, counseling, nutrition as provided by Community Behavioral Health Centers	NA	NA
WI	Combination	Mandated	Developmental disability <21 years of age	$3,000/year per child with disability	Home modifications, child care, counseling, nutrition, clothing, dental/medical, diagnosis/evaluation, equipment, homemaker, home health/nursing, training, recreation, respite, transportation, specialized utility cost, vehicle modification, others as identified and approved	1,300	1,971,000 in 47 of 72 counties
WY	Financial aid	Pilot	Developmental disability 9 children currently in state training school	$350/month 1-time home/vehicle modification	Monthly payment to meet individual expenses for maintaining child at home	9	40,000 (estimated)

bilities and budgeted for in legislative appropriations. The informants in these states spoke of these supports as being a permanent part of the department budget. However, a line item in a departmental budget is somewhat more tenuous than a legislatively mandated program. In 7 states, family supports were small-scale pilots funded by the state department or the developmental disabilities council. Three other states that had either regularly budgeted or mandated services were exploring additional family supports through pilot projects.

The services available to families under the rubric of family support fell into four general categories:

- The oldest and most generally available support was *respite* services. Forty-six states provided some degree of public support for respite for families of children with a developmental disability. In 4 states (Alabama, Delaware, New Mexico, and Vermont), the only state funded family support was respite.
- A total of 36 states funded some other *services* in addition to respite as part of their array of family supports. As we will discuss below, what may be defined as an appropriate family support service varied greatly. In 13 states the support to families was limited to a group of designated services.
- In the last several years increasing attention has been paid to *financial assistance* as a mode for providing flexible family supports. The 25 states that offer some form of financial assistance have developed a number of strategies (see discussion below). Some form of financial assistance was the only state funded family support in 8 states. It should be noted that in the interviews many of these states viewed this assistance as a supplement to services typically available through their general community services.
- Finally, 17 states used some *combination* of financial assistance and services to provide support for families. In general, these two approaches were combined in one of four ways: (a) they may operate as two completely independent programs; (b) the financial assistance may be used to supplement services; (c) the assistance may be targeted to purchasing specific services, such as respite; (d) the financial assistance may be only one component of comprehensive family support and as such may be used to cover expenses not covered or available through the standard array of services.

It was necessary to make a number of judgments to determine whether a state actually had a financial assistance program. Some states listed financial assistance as part of the possible array of family supports but restricted it to assistance for a few allowable expenses such as those associated with making the home accessible. When compared with other states where financial aid is used to purchase essentially anything a family identifies as

TABLE 3.2
Overview of Selected Family Support Practices

STATE	LEGIS-LATION	FINANCIAL ASSISTANCE	SERVICES	FEE FOR SERVICES	RESPITE ONLY	MEDICAID WAIVER	PILOT PROJECT	<100 FAMILIES
AL	—	—	—	X	X	—	X	X
AK	—	—	X	X	—	—	X	X
AZ	—	X	X	X	—	X	—	—
AR	—	X	—	—	—	—	X	X
CA	X	—	X	—	—	X	—	—
CO	—	X	—	—	—	X	—	—
CT	—	X	X	—	—	X	X	X
DE	X	—	—	X	X	X	—	X
FL	X	—	X	—	—	X	—	—
GA	—	—	X	—	—	X	X	—
HI	—	X	—	—	—	—	—	X
ID	—	X	X	—	—	X	—	—
IL	*	X	X	—	—	X	X	—
IN	X	—	X	X	—	—	—	—
IA	X	X	—	—	—	X	—	X
KS	—	—	**	—	—	—	—	—
KY	—	—	X	X	—	—	—	—
LA	*	X	X	—	—	—	X	X
ME	X	—	X	—	—	—	—	X
MD	X	—	X	—	—	—	—	—
MA	X	—	X	—	—	X	—	—
MI	X	X	X	—	—	X	—	—
MN	X	X	X	—	—	X	—	—
MS	—	—	**	—	—	X	**	—
MO	—	—	**	**	—	**	—	—
MT	—	X	X	—	—	X	—	—
NE	X	X	—	—	—	X	—	—
NV	—	X	X	X	—	X	—	X
NH	*	—	X	X	—	—	X	—
NJ	—	—	**	—	—	—	—	—
NM	—	—	—	—	X	—	—	—
NY	—	—	X	—	—	—	—	—
NC	—	—	**	—	—	—	—	—
ND	X	X	X	X	—	X	—	—
OH	X	X	—	X	—	X	—	—
OK	—	—	—	—	—	**	—	—
OR	—	X	X	—	—	X	X	X
PA	—	X	X	—	—	X	—	—
RI	X	X	X	X	—	X	—	X
SC	—	X	X	—	—	X	—	—
SD	—	—	—	—	—	—	—	—
TN	—	—	X	—	—	X	—	X
TX	X	X	—	X	—	—	—	—
UT	—	—	X	—	—	—	—	X
VT	—	—	—	X	X	X	—	—
VA	—	X	X	—	—	—	X	—
WA	X	—	X	—	—	—	—	—
WV	—	—	**	—	—	X	—	—
WI	X	X	X	—	—	X	—	—
WY	—	X	—	—	—	—	X	X
TOTALS	20	25	36	13	4	30	11	15

*These states had new family support legislation that was being implemented at the time of the study. **Although these states did not identify family support as a specific priority, some services were available to families.

a need, this limited approach seemed to fall short of a true financial assistance program. For this reason, states with significant restrictions are not listed as having a financial assistance component in their family support system.

A final important component of a state's efforts in family support is the degree to which it uses options available under Medicaid to provide for care in the family home. The issue of state approaches to Medicaid policy will be addressed below. Here and in Table 3.2, we are only looking for an indication that the state had given some thought about the relationship between Medicaid policy and support for families by at least developing a single Medicaid waiver. An "X" in the Medicaid waiver column on Table 3.2 indicates that the state had at least a "Model 50" fragile waiver in place. These waivers allow states to develop targeted programs for families caring for medically fragile children. Based on our interviews, 30 states met this criteria. It should be noted that in the cases of Oklahoma and Missouri, the family support aspects of the waiver were secondary to a primary focus on community services for adults. Also, in West Virginia and Mississippi the options available under the Medicaid waiver were the principal family support activity in the state.

Number of Families Served

The limited availability of family supports in most states becomes readily apparent when the number of families actually receiving support is examined. The number of families covered in each state ranged from 9 in Wyoming to approximately 25,000 in California. As the last column in Table 3.2 indicates, in 15 states the major components of the family support program served less than 100 families. Data reported by the 5 states with the largest family support efforts, California, New York (24,000), Pennsylvania (15,000), Florida (11,336), and Massachusetts (10,000), should be more closely examined to determine how many families were actually receiving services beyond nominal case management and maintenance on the eligibility rolls.

Eligibility Criteria

Most states have adopted relatively broad eligibility criteria for their family support efforts. As shown in column 3 in Table 3.1, the principal criterion in most instances was a diagnosis of a developmental disability. A few states have adopted a program-specific definition of eligibility for their family supports. These latter criteria generally seem to be efforts to avoid the restrictions inherent in categorical approaches to eligibility. For example, Louisiana's criteria for respite services included as eligible a person with a chronic physical or mental disability that (a) is not primarily the result of the aging process, (b) is likely to continue indefinitely, and (c) results in limitation in three major life areas. In 9 instances, states have adopted more restrictive eligibility criteria by using a narrow categorical definition of developmental disability or by limiting eligibility to one or a few diagnostic categories.

The other principal strategy for controlling eligibility for family supports is to attach conditions in addition to the presence of a disability. Five states limited eligibility for some aspect of their family support effort to people with severe disabilities. To define this term, states typically highlight functional limitations in a large number of life areas or, in Michigan and Iowa, allow "severe" disability to be defined by the state's education regulations. Nine states forego the use of a categorical approach to eligibility in favor of one based on current life situation. In these latter cases the program was usually defined as intervening to alleviate a "crisis" or to prevent an out-of-home placement.

Although a large number of states indicated that their family support efforts were primarily targeted on families with minor children, only 12 states limited eligibility for family supports to that group. So, in most cases, these programs allowed for what can more appropriately be termed "in-home and family supports" since their primary focus seems to be offering the supports which people, adults and children, with a disability need to live in a family situation. In most states, the definition of family used was very flexible. In practice, our interviews indicated that the programs look at the quality of the relationship of the people in the household to determine whether a particular living arrangement constitutes a home and family. In Hawaii, for example, a family is defined as a person living with a parent (birth or adopted), sibling, spouse, son, daughter, grandparent, aunt or uncle, cousin, guardian, or a person who has become a member of an immediate family through the custom of "Hanai." In most states the major restriction imposed by the relevant laws and regulations was the exclusion of foster homes or other situations involving paid caregivers. But even this restriction was by no means universal, and several states specifically included foster homes as eligible. This difference in policy seemed to be associated with the level of support in each state for foster care. States with low foster care reimbursement rates seemed to look to family support funds as a way of enhancing their rates and thereby creating a form of specialized foster care for people with disabilities.

The final major factor that is considered in determining program eligibility is family income. Thirteen states, especially those that offer some kind of direct financial assistance, also had income based restrictions on eligibility. The standard used in this determination can vary from some absolute ceiling established by the law or regulations (range: an annual income of $30,000 in Georgia to $60,000 in Michigan) to a measure tied to some changing indicator, such as a percentage of the state's median income. Additionally, 13 of the state respondents interviewed indicated that there was a fee for service attached to some or all aspects of their family support program. In most of these cases, people at the lower end of a sliding scale pay nothing for services and at the upper end the family pays a substantial portion of the cost.

Services Covered and Allowable Expenditures

There is wide variation in the type and range of services and supports that states describe as family supports. Table 3.3 indicates which of 38 "services" are identified by each state as part of its system of family support. Because of state differences in service definitions, many of the services listed in the first column of Table 3.3 reflect the inclusion of a range of closely related service categories. As noted above, respite is the only service that was universally identified as a family support. The next most frequently identified supports, adaptive equipment (31 states) and family counseling (27 states), were found in roughly two thirds of the states. No other supports were identified by more than 50% of the states.

The range of support services available in any one state varies from none to 27 allowable services (Louisiana and Wisconsin). The last two "services" listed in column 1 of Table 3.3 merit some mention because they are often used to provide the flexibility that is a key characteristic of the emerging definition of family support. In the 24 states that used these two options, the list of available services described in state law or regulations is open-ended and is prefaced by a phrase such as the following: "Family support services shall include but not be limited to the following services." The list of mandated services is usually followed by a section that outlines a family support planning process which allows the family to identify either "other support needs" or "other disability related expenses or services not covered by other sources" which can then be identified as part of the array of supports for an individual family.

A careful examination of the services catalogued in Table 3.3 makes it clear that a number of different types of services are grouped under the general rubric of family support. We suggest that this diversity can be better organized by viewing publicly subsidized family supports as being made up of three principal components: services, case management, and financial assistance. Within each of these broad categories are a number of subordinate service categories or approaches. Table 3.4 organizes the family support activities described in our inquiries into related categories of support.

TABLE 3.3
Services Provided or Covered by State Family Support Programs

SERVICES[a]	AL	AK	AZ	AR	CA	CO	CT	DE	FL	GA	HI	ID	IL
Respite	X	X	X	X	X	X	X	X	X	X	X	X	X
Adaptive equipment	—	—	X	X	X	X	—	—	X	X	X	X	—
Family counseling	—	—	—	—	X	X	—	—	X	X	X	X	—
Occupational therapy[b]	—	—	—	—	—	X	—	—	X	X	—	X	—
Parent training	—	X	X	—	X	X	—	—	—	X	X	—	—
Physical therapy[b]	—	—	—	—	—	X	—	—	X	X	—	X	—
Behavior management[b]	—	—	—	—	X	X	—	—	X	X	—	—	—
Case management	—	—	X	—	—	X	X	—	X	X	—	—	X
Speech therapy[b]	—	—	—	—	—	X	—	—	X	X	—	X	—
Home modification	—	—	X	X	—	—	—	—	X	—	X	X	—
Voucher/Reimbursement	—	—	X	X	—	X	—	—	—	—	X	X	X
Transportation	—	—	X	—	—	X	—	—	X	X	X	X	—
Homemaker	—	—	X	—	X	X	—	—	—	X	X	—	—
Individual counseling[b]	—	—	—	—	X	—	—	—	X	X	—	—	—
Medical/Dental[b]	—	—	—	—	X	—	—	—	X	X	X	X	—
Skill training[b]	—	X	—	—	—	X	—	—	X	X	—	—	—
Special diet	—	—	—	—	—	X	—	—	X	X	—	X	—
Attendant care	—	X	—	X	—	—	—	—	—	X	—	—	—
Evaluation/Assessment[b]	—	—	—	—	—	—	—	—	X	X	—	X	—
Home health care	—	—	X	—	—	X	—	—	—	X	—	X	—
Child care	—	—	—	—	X	X	—	—	X	—	—	X	—
Special clothing	—	—	—	X	—	X	—	—	X	X	—	X	—
Recreation	—	—	—	—	—	X	—	—	—	X	—	X	—
Cash subsidy	—	—	—	—	—	—	X	—	—	—	—	—	X
Family support groups	—	—	—	—	—	—	—	—	—	—	—	X	—
Nursing[b]	—	—	X	—	—	—	—	—	—	X	—	—	—
Information/Referral	—	—	—	—	—	—	—	—	—	—	—	—	—
Sitter service	—	—	X	—	X	X	—	—	—	X	—	—	—
Vehicle modification	—	—	—	—	—	—	—	—	—	—	—	—	—
Advocacy	—	—	—	—	X	—	—	—	—	—	—	—	—
Camp	X	—	—	—	X	—	—	—	—	—	—	—	—
Utilities	—	—	—	—	—	—	—	—	—	—	—	—	—
Chores	—	—	X	—	—	—	—	—	—	—	—	—	—
Health insurance	—	—	—	—	—	—	—	—	—	—	—	—	—
Home repairs	—	—	X	—	—	—	—	—	—	—	—	—	—
Rent assistance	—	—	X	—	—	—	—	—	—	—	—	—	—
Disability-related expenses not covered by others	—	—	—	—	—	—	X	—	—	—	X	—	—
Other as identified	—	X	—	X	X	X	—	—	X	X	—	X	X
TOTAL	2	5	14	7	13	20	4	1	18	23	10	18	5

[a] Services are listed according to frequency of availability. [b] Indicates a traditional developmental service that has been included as a family support because it can be "delivered" in the home.

TABLE 3.3 Services Provided or Covered by State Family Support Programs *(Continued)*

SERVICES[a]	IN	IA	KS	KY	LA	ME	MD	MA	MI	MN	MS	MO	MT
Respite	X	—	X	X	X	X	X	X	X	X	—	X	X
Adaptive equipment	X	—	—	—	X	—	X	X	X	X	—	X	X
Family counseling	X	—	—	—	X	X	—	X	X	—	X	X	X
Occupational therapy[b]	—	—	—	X	X	X	—	X	X	X	X	—	X
Parent training	—	—	X	—	X	X	—	—	X	—	X	—	X
Physical therapy[b]	—	—	—	X	X	X	—	X	X	X	X	—	X
Behavior management[b]	X	—	—	X	X	X	X	X	X	X	X	X	—
Case management	X	—	X	X	X	X	—	—	X	X	X	—	X
Speech therapy[b]	—	—	—	X	X	—	—	X	X	X	X	—	X
Home modification	—	—	—	—	X	—	—	—	—	—	—	—	X
Voucher/ Reimbursement	X	—	—	—	X	—	—	—	—	X	—	—	X
Transportation	X	—	—	—	X	X	X	X	—	X	—	—	—
Homemaker	X	—	—	—	X	—	—	X	—	X	—	—	X
Individual counseling[b]	—	—	—	—	X	—	—	X	X	—	—	X	X
Medical/Dental[b]	X	—	—	—	X	—	—	—	—	—	—	—	X
Skill training[b]	X	—	—	—	—	—	—	—	—	—	—	—	X
Special diet	X	—	—	—	X	—	—	—	—	—	—	—	—
Attendant care	X	—	—	X	X	—	—	X	—	—	—	—	X
Evaluation/Assessment[b]	—	—	—	—	X	X	—	—	X	X	X	—	X
Home health care	—	—	—	—	X	—	—	—	—	—	—	X	—
Child care	—	—	—	—	X	—	—	—	—	X	—	—	X
Special clothing	X	—	—	—	X	—	—	—	—	—	—	—	—
Recreation	—	—	—	—	X	X	—	X	—	—	—	—	—
Cash subsidy	—	X	—	—	X	—	—	—	X	—	—	—	—
Family support groups	—	—	—	—	X	X	—	X	X	—	—	—	X
Nursing[b]	—	—	—	—	X	—	—	—	—	X	—	X	—
Information/Referral	—	—	X	—	—	—	—	X	X	—	—	—	X
Sitter service	—	—	—	—	—	—	—	—	X	—	—	—	—
Vehicle modification	—	—	—	—	X	—	X	—	—	—	—	—	—
Advocacy	—	—	—	—	—	X	—	—	—	—	—	—	X
Camp	—	—	—	—	—	—	—	—	—	—	—	—	—
Utilities	—	—	—	—	X	—	—	—	—	—	—	—	—
Chores	—	—	—	—	—	—	—	—	—	—	—	—	—
Health insurance	—	—	—	—	—	—	—	—	—	—	—	—	—
Home repairs	—	—	—	—	—	—	—	—	—	—	—	—	—
Rent assistance	—	—	—	—	—	—	—	—	—	—	—	—	—
Disability-related expenses not covered by others	—	—	—	—	—	—	—	—	—	X	—	—	—
Other as identified	X	—	—	X	—	—	—	—	X	—	—	—	X
TOTAL	14	1	4	8	27	12	5	14	16	14	8	7	21

[a] Services are listed according to frequency of availability. [b] Indicates a traditional developmental service that has been included as a family support because it can be "delivered" in the home.

STATE PROGRAMS 79

TABLE 3.3 Services Provided or Covered by State Family Support Programs *(Continued)*

SERVICES[a]	NE	NV	NH	NJ	NM	NY	NC	ND	OH	OK	OR	PA	RI
Respite	X	X	X	X	X	X	X	X	X	X	X	X	X
Adaptive equipment	X	—	X	X	—	X	—	X	X	—	X	X	X
Family counseling	X	—	—	—	—	X	—	X	X	—	X	—	X
Occupational therapy[b]	—	—	X	—	—	X	—	X	—	—	—	X	X
Parent training	X	—	X	—	—	X	—	X	X	—	X	X	X
Physical therapy[b]	—	—	X	—	—	X	—	X	—	—	—	X	X
Behavior management[b]	—	—	X	—	—	X	—	X	—	—	—	X	—
Case management	—	X	X	X	—	X	—	—	—	X	—	—	X
Speech therapy[b]	—	—	X	—	—	X	—	X	—	—	—	X	X
Home modification	X	—	X	—	—	X	—	X	X	—	X	X	X
Voucher/Reimbursement	X	—	X	—	—	X	—	X	X	—	X	X	X
Transportation	X	—	—	—	—	X	—	X	—	—	X	—	—
Homemaker	X	—	—	—	—	—	—	X	—	X	—	X	X
Individual counseling[b]	X	—	—	—	—	X	—	X	—	—	X	—	—
Medical/Dental[b]	—	—	—	—	—	—	—	X	X	—	X	X	X
Skill training[b]	X	—	—	—	—	X	—	X	X	X	X	—	—
Special diet	—	—	—	—	—	X	—	X	X	—	X	X	—
Attendant care	X	—	—	—	—	—	—	—	—	—	X	—	—
Evaluation/Assessment[b]	—	—	—	—	—	X	—	—	—	X	—	—	—
Home health care	X	—	—	—	—	—	—	X	—	—	X	—	X
Child care	—	X	—	—	—	X	—	X	—	—	—	—	—
Special clothing	—	—	—	—	—	—	—	X	—	—	X	—	—
Recreation	—	—	—	—	—	X	—	X	—	—	—	X	—
Cash subsidy	—	X	—	—	—	—	—	—	—	—	—	X	—
Family support groups	—	—	—	—	—	X	—	—	—	—	—	—	X
Nursing[b]	—	—	—	—	—	—	—	—	—	—	—	—	—
Information/Referral	—	—	X	—	—	X	X	—	—	—	—	—	—
Sitter service	—	—	—	—	—	—	—	—	—	—	—	X	—
Vehicle modification	—	—	—	—	—	—	—	—	—	—	X	—	—
Advocacy	—	—	—	—	—	X	—	—	—	—	—	—	—
Camp	—	—	—	—	—	—	—	—	—	—	—	—	—
Utilities	—	—	—	—	—	—	—	—	—	—	—	—	—
Chores	—	—	—	—	—	—	—	—	—	—	—	—	—
Health insurance	—	—	—	—	—	—	—	X	—	—	—	—	—
Home repairs	—	—	—	—	—	—	—	—	—	—	—	—	—
Rent assistance	—	—	—	—	—	—	—	—	—	—	—	—	—
Disability-related expenses not covered by others	—	—	—	—	—	—	—	—	—	—	—	—	—
Other as identified	—	—	X	—	—	X	—	—	—	—	—	—	X
TOTAL	12	4	12	3	1	22	2	21	9	5	15	15	15

[a] Services are listed according to frequency of availability. [b] Indicates a traditional developmental service that has been included as a family support because it can be "delivered" in the home.

TABLE 3.3 Services Provided or Covered by State Family Support Programs *(Continued)*

SERVICES[a]	SC	SD	TN	TX	UT	VT	VA	WA	WV	WI	WY	No. of states allowing service
Respite	X	—	X	X	X	X	X	X	X	X	—	46
Adaptive equipment	—	—	X	X	X	—	X	X	—	X	—	31
Family counseling	X	—	X	X	X	X	—	—	X	X	—	27
Occupational therapy[b]	X	—	X	X	X	—	—	X	X	X	—	24
Parent training	X	—	—	X	X	—	—	—	—	X	—	24
Physical therapy[b]	X	—	X	X	X	—	—	X	X	X	—	24
Behavior management[b]	—	—	—	X	X	X	X	X	—	X	—	24
Case management	X	—	—	—	—	—	—	—	—	X	—	23
Speech therapy[b]	X	—	X	X	X	—	—	X	X	X	—	23
Home modification	X	—	X	X	—	—	X	X	—	X	X	22
Voucher/Reimbursement	—	—	—	X	—	—	X	—	—	X	—	21
Transportation	—	—	X	X	—	—	—	—	—	X	—	19
Homemaker	—	—	—	X	X	—	—	—	—	X	—	18
Individual counseling[b]	—	—	—	X	X	X	—	—	X	X	—	17
Medical/Dental[b]	—	—	X	X	—	—	X	—	—	X	—	17
Skill training[b]	X	—	—	X	X	—	—	—	—	X	—	16
Special diet	—	—	X	—	X	—	—	—	X	X	—	15
Attendant care	—	—	—	X	X	—	—	X	—	X	—	14
Evaluation/Assessment[b]	X	—	—	X	—	—	—	—	—	X	—	14
Home health care	—	—	X	X	X	—	—	—	—	X	—	14
Child care	—	—	X	—	—	—	—	—	—	X	—	12
Special clothing	—	—	X	X	—	—	—	—	—	X	—	12
Recreation	—	—	X	—	—	—	—	—	—	X	—	11
Cash subsidy	X	—	—	—	—	—	—	—	—	—	X	9
Family support groups	X	—	—	—	—	—	—	—	—	—	—	9
Nursing[b]	—	—	X	X	X	—	—	—	—	X	—	9
Information/Referral	—	—	—	—	—	—	X	—	—	—	—	8
Sitter service	—	—	X	—	—	—	—	—	—	—	—	7
Vehicle modification	—	—	X	—	—	—	X	—	—	X	X	7
Advocacy	—	—	X	—	—	—	—	—	—	—	—	5
Camp	X	—	X	—	—	—	—	—	—	—	—	4
Utilities	—	—	—	—	—	—	—	—	—	X	—	2
Chores	—	—	—	—	—	—	—	—	—	—	—	1
Health insurance	—	—	—	—	—	—	—	—	—	—	—	1
Home repairs	—	—	—	—	—	—	—	—	—	—	—	1
Rent assistance	—	—	—	—	—	—	—	—	—	—	—	1
Disability-related expenses not covered by others	—	—	—	—	—	—	—	—	—	—	—	3
Other as identified	—	—	X	X	X	—	X	X	X	X	—	22
TOTAL	13	0	20	21	16	4	9	9	8	27	3	

[a] Services are listed according to frequency of availability. [b] Indicates a traditional developmental service that has been included as a family support because it can be "delivered" in the home.

TABLE 4
Taxonomy of Family Support

SERVICES

CORE SERVICES

Respite and child care:
  Respite
  Child care
  Sitter services

Recreation:
  Recreation
  Camp

Supportive:
  Family counseling
  Family support groups
  Siblings groups

Training:
  Parent training

In-home assistance:
  Homemaker
  Attendant care
  Home health care
  Chores

Environmental adaptations:
  Adaptive equipment
  Home modifications
  Vehicle modification

Systemic assistance:
  Information and referral
  Advocacy

Extra-ordinary/ordinary needs:
  Transportation
  Special diet
  Special clothing
  Utilities
  Health insurance
  Home repairs
  Rent assistance

TRADITIONAL DEVELOPMENTAL SERVICES
  Behavior management
  Speech therapy
  Occupational therapy
  Physical therapy
  Individual counseling
  Medical/Dental
  Skill training
  Evaluation/Assessment
  Nursing

CASE MANAGEMENT/SERVICE COORDINATION

FINANCIAL ASSISTANCE
  Discretionary cash subsidy
  Allowances
  Vouchers
  Reimbursement
  Line of credit

Services

An initial problem in organizing the data collected in the interviews was the need to decide what was appropriately called a family support service. A number of states with very limited family support efforts provided extensive descriptions of their efforts in early intervention under PL

99-457. While the mandate for integration and a family centered approach in this law are completely congruent with the emerging approach to supporting families, we decided not to consider early intervention as synonymous with family support. This decision was based on the premise that access to these services is restricted to a discrete age group and the primary focus is on prevention and amelioration of disability rather than on long-term support of the family unit.

Traditional Developmental Services. At least nine of the most frequently identified services fell into the category of traditional developmental services that many school-age children receive as related services through their school program or that are available through community based disability agencies or regional service centers. These 9 services have a distinctly different focus from the other 24 services identified as family supports. Core family supports can be characterized by their focus on the family as a whole, while those listed under traditional developmental services are individually centered, clinical interventions usually outlined in an individualized plan of service. They become "family supports" when a state makes provisions for them to be delivered in the home.

Core Family Supports. The supports in this category reflect the guiding values of family-focused, parent-controlled, flexible, and community-based—values that are intrinsic in the emerging approach to supporting families. They fall into the eight distinct categories shown in Table 3.4.

1. *Respite and child care* are the most widely available support service, with 46 states making some provision in this area. As with most supports, there is wide variability in what is actually available to families. In some states, this service may be restricted to one form of respite no more than 10 days a year. Yet other states provide for a variety of respite options, child care support, and assistance in finding sitters services for both the child with the disability and children without a disability.

2. *Environmental adaptation* is provided in 32 states. This category of support ranges from states where the public sector completely covers the costs associated with making a home fully accessible and obtaining adaptive equipment to states where partial reimbursement is provided for a portion of the costs associated with these needs.

3. *Supportive services* are provided in 27 states. These supports can take multiple forms ranging from traditional individual counseling for parents to self-help groups including family support groups, sibling groups, and family counseling services.

4. *In-home assistance* is allowed in some form in 26 states. This mode of support provides for outside assistance to either (a) help in the care of the person with a disability, so the prime caregiver can look to the other needs of the family or (b) assist with the typical household activities, so family members can see to the needs of the family member with a disability.

5. *Extraordinary/ordinary needs* are covered in 26 states. There is extreme variability here, particularly since states with cash subsidy programs or very flexible voucher programs see these needs as being covered by those funding mechanisms. Even states with less flexible approaches, however, recognize the fact that the specialized needs of a child with a disability may substantially increase the cost of rent, health insurance, utilities, food, clothing, and so forth.

6. *Training* for parents and other family members is covered in 24 states. This training can vary widely in focus, from information related to disability to information related to individual advocacy and systems change.

7. *Recreation* is an allowable family support activity in 14 states. In some states this takes the form of special camps and special recreation programs, but in an increasing number of states this activity assists families to gain access to the recreational resources that are typically available in their communities.

8. *Systemic assistance* is identified in 11 states as a family support service. This category includes the provision of information to families about the resources that are available to them and, in at least 5 states, direct assistance to assure that families receive all of the services to which they have a right. In several of these latter states, this advocacy activity is consciously aimed at moving other components of the service system into line with family-centered principles.

In summary, 30 states provide at least one family support service in four or more of the *core* categories outlined above. Of these states, 20 also provide the majority of the traditional developmental services as part of their family supports. A total of 24 states provide the majority of the traditional services as in-home and family supports. Six states provide seven of the eight core supports as a permanent part of their family supports. It is worth noting that of those states with no formalized family support system, Missouri allows for most of the core family supports as part of its community services. On the other hand, the state of Washington has a clear family support mandate, yet provides for few of the core services and concentrates its effort on providing traditional services.

Case Management

Case management is distinguished from all other services because of its role as the linchpin for all other services and supports that a family may need or desire. The literature on community services in general and family support in particular consistently underscores this unique and crucial role. Our interviews confirm the importance of case management. In most of the 23 states that identified case management as a family support, it is the only mandated service that all families can be sure they will receive. Unfortunately, the mere availability of case management as a mandated service tells very little about the way in which it is carried out. In general, there are two very different approaches to case management.

The first variation is the traditional approach to case management. The case manager, with a large caseload fulfills an assessment and referral function. He or she listens as the family outlines their needs, or they fill out an evaluation questionnaire based on their qualitative assessment. The case manager then describes what services are available, who is eligible to receive the services, and at what cost. From this array, ideally, the family can choose what they need. In actuality, they often have to accept whatever is offered. In some cases, families are put on waiting lists, referred to other agencies or simply denied services. The case manager has the job of telling the parents not only what they need, but what they can have. Families can say what they need, but are ultimately told what they can have. To many parents this is not family support or case management but management of the family by a professional.

The second variation is case management that assists the family to determine and direct "family support" activities. In this role, the professional helps the family to identify the long and short term support services they need and assists them to gain access to these services. If the services do not exist, then the case manager works to find them or provides the technical assistance to generic, community based agencies to create the service or augment already existing services.

Financial Assistance

The third major component in the emerging system of family supports is financial assistance to families of people with disabilities. The way in which this type of support is administered can have an immense influence on other aspects of the system of supports. A few states see financial assistance as the essence of their approach to family support. As a consequence, these states impose few restrictions on the use of funds, and have the expectation that families will use them to purchase whatever services and supports they need. These states are likely to have very few publicly subsidized services available. A second group of states, somewhat "richer" in services, provide financial assistance in the form of service vouchers which families can then use to make purchases from the available range of services. A third approach in some states that have an extensive array of formal services involves using financial aid to allow families to obtain supports beyond those the state offers. However, this approach is coupled with significant restrictions on what families are allowed to purchase. The final approach to financial assistance is very open-ended and allows families to determine their own needs. This approach is distinguished from the first approach described because it is associated with an extensive array of publicly subsidized services. Financial assistance in these latter states is seen as a way of meeting the unique needs of each family.

The five strategies for providing financial assistance listed in Table 3.4 are not necessarily mutually exclusive; several states either use or are experimenting with many of these approaches. In addition, none of these strategies is tied to any one of the four approaches to financial assistance outlined in the previous paragraph. The first strategy, cash subsidy, is used in the 9 states indicated on Table 3.3. The other four methods are used alone or in combination in the 21 states which Table 3.3 indicates use "Voucher/Reimbursement."

1. *Discretionary cash subsidy.* This method of providing financial assistance involves providing a family with a regular payment of a set amount of cash to defray the extra cost of raising a child with a disability. Most states that have adopted this strategy give the family a monthly payment that is roughly equivalent to that state's SSI payment for an adult with a disability. The family may be required to provide receipts to document the use of the subsidy.

2. *Allowances.* This strategy is distinct from the first and usually involves the use of vouchers or reimbursement for expenses. As a rule, the amount of cash is less than a direct subsidy. For example, a family may be allotted a monthly allowance to cover the cost of respite, medication, food, clothing, or transportation. Usually families are required to provide receipts for the full amount of the allowance.

3. *Vouchers.* This method is most often used to provide and control access to specialized services such as respite. A family is allocated vouchers for a specific amount of services. The vouchers are then given to the provider, who is paid by the state agency. In some cases, families can use their own cash to purchase services in excess of their voucher amount. In other cases, families can only obtain the amount of services for which they have vouchers. A few states have used vouchers to arrange for such things as home adaptations, medication, or food (through arrangements that parallel food stamps) with community merchants.

4. *Reimbursement.* Under this method, families pay for covered goods and services. They then submit their receipts to the family support program, which reimburses them for all or part of their expenditures.

5. *Line of credit.* This variant of the voucher system has been tried in Texas. Families involved in the program are issued a bank card with a monthly credit limit that they can use to cover the cost of services or supports with participating providers, who bill against the balance remaining in the family's account.

Limitations on Benefits to Individual Families

An important concern to families is the extent of limitations placed on the amount of supports available to them. The "Limitations on Benefits" column in Table 3.1 shows that, as in other aspects of family support, state practices varied widely. Most respite programs had a limitation imposed on the number of days available for a period of 6 months or a year. This restriction ranged from 10 to 60 days per year. An examination of the funds allocated to the 16 discrete respite programs indicates that on average a family gets about $1,000 worth of respite services per year. This benefit ranges from $300 in Nevada to $2,222 in Maine. However, these findings must be interpreted carefully. Several interviewees indicated that because of the limited number of providers available, families are rarely able to obtain the amount of respite to which they are "entitled," let alone exceed that allocation.

We examined 23 separate programs in the 19 states that provided some form of direct financial assistance to families. The limitations on benefits in these programs ranged from about $2,000 to $5,000 per year. When the number of families served by a program is compared with the funds allocated to that program, the actual average benefit during the fiscal period covered in the study averages $2,838 with a range from almost $410 in Iowa to $5,556 in Arkansas. This wide discrepancy reflects programs that were just getting started and so were funding some families for only a fraction of the year. In addition, our data collection on cost did not separate the overhead cost associated with a program from the direct benefits obtained by families.

Many of the states that provided a combination of services and financial assistance or only services indicated that services and limits are individually determined. An admittedly rough measure is average benefits based on number of families served and program allocation. This approach, however, does not include an overhead cost which is included in the cost of other family support efforts. Within these constraints, we examined the 23 service programs found in 22 states. The average family benefit under this approach is $2,923. The range here is from $342 in Kentucky to $12,478 in Montana's specialized home care program, which provides intensive supports to birth, adoptive, and foster families.

Current Funding Levels

State efforts in the area of family support varied from the $37,880 provided by the Wyoming Developmental Disabilities Council for a pilot project to return nine institutionalized children to their homes, to the $30,511,839 allocated by the California legislature to provide in-home and family support through that state's system of regional centers. In the 45 states that clearly committed a portion of their budget to family supports, the average allocation was $3,826,623 for a national total of $172,198,035. When compared to the national budget of $11,716,825,830 for services for people with mental retardation and developmental disabilities (Braddock et al., 1990), the family support commitment amounts to approximately 1.5% of total expenditures to support approximately 129,777 families.

In an effort to find a measure of state family support efforts that makes some allowance for differences in population and income level across the country, we settled on the state's gross personal income. Table 3.5 presents these data. The first column in this table indicates the state's family support ranking based on the number of dollars committed to family support (column 3) per thousand dollars of gross personal income (column 4). The result of this computation is found in column 5. As a comparison measure, the figure in parentheses next to the personal income figure indicates how each state ranks on per capita income. The average effort on family supports in the 45 states with programs of some kind is $0.05 per thousand dollars of personal income (SD = $0.078, range $0.44 to $0.0017).

Program Structure

In order to explore the degree to which ideals such as easy access, parent-professional partnership, program flexibility, and a strong parent role in the planning and oversight of family support programs are being realized, the informants were asked to describe how their state's family support efforts were structured. In this section we briefly summarize the eight major structural components associated with family support that were consistently described in the interviews. None of these individual components guarantees that the ideals of a parent-controlled family-centered approach will be realized. It does seem, however, that the more energy a state or region devotes to these complex issues, the higher likelihood that it will have a well articulated system of family supports.

1. *Regional control.* At least 32 states indicated that their approach to family supports placed a great deal of control at the regional or county level. In some cases, this control is on the level of managing distribution of benefits or providing services; in others the regions or counties, because of their degree of fiscal and programmatic autonomy, actually define what family support means in their area. The positive side of this practice places control of resources closer to families. The down side of this approach is it leads to a great deal of regional variation in the benefits available to families.

2. *Central role of case management.* In at least 23 states a person called a case manager plays a central role in the system of family supports. An

TABLE 3.5
State Family Support Effort per $1,000 of Personal Income

RANK	STATE	TOTAL FAMILY SUPPORT EFFORT ($)	PERSONAL INCOME IN $1,000[a]	FAMILY SUPPORT PER $1,000 OF PERSONAL INCOME ($)
1	North Dakota	3,977,000	9,000,000 (36)	0.4419
2	Montana	2,547,203	10,000,000 (42)	0.2547
3	New Hampshire	3,712,270	20,000,000 (4)	0.1856
4	Massachusetts	18,500,000	117,000,000 (3)	0.1581
5	Rhode Island	1,867,000	16,000,000 (17)	0.1167
6	Michigan	14,679,251	149,000,000 (18)	0.0985
7	Maine	1,500,000	17,000,000 (31)	0.0882
8	Alaska	718,000	10,000,000 (7)	0.0718
9	New York	22,500,000	327,000,000 (8)	0.0688
10	Vermont	544,150	8,000,000 (29)	0.0680
11	Pennsylvania	12,000,000	188,000,000 (21)	0.0638
12	California	30,511,839	511,000,000 (6)	0.0597
13	Florida	11,285,234	195,000,000 (14)	0.0579
14	New Jersey[b]	8,793,000	163,000,000 (2)	0.0539
15	Missouri[b]	3,638,053	77,000,000 (24)	0.0472
16	Arizona	2,349,600	50,000,000 (25)	0.0470
17	Maryland	4,000,000	86,000,000 (5)	0.0465
18	Louisiana[c]	1,804,378	52,000,000 (48)	0.0347
19	Washington	2,500,000	74,000,000 (16)	0.0338
20	Ohio	4,777,305	162,000,000 (26)	0.0295
21	Wisconsin	1,971,000	73,000,000 (23)	0.0270
22	Kentucky[b]	1,211,814	47,000,000 (40)	0.0258
23	Illinois[c]	4,720,000	197,000,000 (12)	0.0240
24	Utah	447,100	20,000,000 (44)	0.0224
25	Connecticut	1,373,472	71,000,000 (1)	0.0193
26	Texas	4,315,000	241,000,000 (32)	0.0179
27	Minnesota	1,128,700	70,000,000 (15)	0.0161
28	Nevada	244,478	17,000,000 (9)	0.0144
29	Arkansas	400,000	28,000,000 (47)	0.0143
30	Nebraska	300,000	24,000,000 (27)	0.0125
31	New Mexico	187,000	18,000,000 (43)	0.0104
32	Idaho	120,000	12,000,000 (45)	0.0100
33	Iowa	400,000	41,000,000 (33)	0.0098
34	North Carolina[b]	812,311	89,000,000 (34)	0.0091
35	Oregon[c]	305,000	40,000,000 (28)	0.0076
36	Delaware	75,000	11,000,000 (11)	0.0068
37	Georgia	611,562	92,000,000 (22)	0.0066
38	Colorado	343,000	53,000,000 (19)	0.0065
39	Hawaii	115,000	18,000,000 (13)	0.0064
40	Alabama[c]	325,000	51,000,000 (41)	0.0064
41	Wyoming[c]	37,800	6,000,000 (46)	0.0063
42	Indiana	434,535	80,000,000 (30)	0.0054
43	South Carolina	220,000	43,000,000 (37)	0.0051
44	Virginia	175,000	102,000,000 (10)	0.0017
45	Tennessee	108,000	64,000,000 (35)	0.0017
46	Mississippi		28,000,000 (50)	0.0000
47	West Virginia		21,000,000 (49)	0.0000
48	Oklahoma		42,000,000 (39)	0.0000
49	South Dakota		9,000,000 (38)	0.0000
50	Kansas		39,000,000 (20)	0.0000

[a] The parenthetical numbers show the states' relative ranking based on per capita income.
[b] While not a family support initiative, a portion of these funds provides services to families.
[c] A portion of this state's family support effort is financed with Developmental Disabilities Council funds.

awareness of a need for professional expertise to assist families in obtaining benefits and services underlies this role. However, there is extreme state to state variability in how the role associated with this job title is defined. In some cases, the role is only nominal, as people with massive caseloads do little more than occasionally refer families (usually those in crisis) to potential services. In other states, the case manager is in a very strong position and actually determines what benefits a family needs and gets. Finally, in a small but increasing number of states, the person works in close collaboration with families as their guide through the complexities of the service system.

3. *Parent advisory boards.* Eighteen states attempt to respond to parents and family members by assuring that they have a high degree of visibility and have a voice on the advisory boards that oversee state and local family support efforts. In some instances these boards are really only advisory in nature, although most of the informants indicated that the policy makers do listen to them. In several states, these boards are more than merely advisory and are empowered to make policy for the family support program.

4. *Individualized family support planning process.* Obviously some sort of planning process is associated with every family support effort. Seventeen states have an individualized family support planning process that every eligible family goes through before receiving benefits. Some of these processes are an extension of the Individualized Program Plan which was required for the family member with a disability. Others are, in fact, field tests of the planning process to be used in the state's implementation of PL 99-457. A number of states have developed a process that is specific to their family support effort and focuses on attempting to actualize the ideal of family control.

5. *True decision-making in the hands of parents.* This policy or practice may on its face seem somehow redundant, given the description of some of the emerging family-centered approaches to case management, planning, and the role of family advisory boards, but 15 states have felt compelled to mandate this in the laws, regulations, or guidelines for their family support effort.

6. *Use of local agencies.* This approach to services is different from the regionalized approach mentioned above. It points more to a privatization of family support efforts, since 12 states use local private for-profit and not-for-profit agencies as their principal vehicles for managing or providing family supports. In a very few cases, this effort has led states to expand beyond traditional specialized services to use the generic resources of the community as principal family support resources.

7. *An appeal process.* Five states have established a process for families to appeal any dispute they may have regarding determination of eligibility or other aspects of family support practice to a higher authority.

8. *A mechanism for quality assurance.* Only five states indicated that they have established or were planning to establish a formal mechanism to assure that services provided as family support met certain minimum standards of quality. Most states left the entire issue of quality exclusively in the hands of families with little or no recourse other than to either find a new provider or discontinue receiving a service if they feel it was of poor quality.

Implementation Issues

To highlight some of the practical concerns that any state must address in developing a family support effort, the informants were asked to discuss the issues that have caused the greatest difficulty in their state. The way an issue is expressed varied greatly from state to state and some states had a long list of issues. Nevertheless, eight major issues were consistently noted by interviewees. Here we will briefly outline these recurring implementation issues.

1. *Demand versus availability.* Twenty states noted that family supports have been very well received and extremely successful but that the resources allocated to these programs were nowhere near adequate to meet the current need. In some states, it was a simple matter of underfunding, which was variously attributed to the competing demands on funding by facilities such as group homes or institutions or to a continuing reticence on the part of the legislature to actively provide public funds for families. In several states, the difference between demand and availability merely reflected the success of a pilot program that had been an effective vehicle for promoting family supports. As a result of the pilot's successes, families throughout the state were clamoring for similar services.

2. *Eligibility.* This second major issue is somewhat connected to the first. In at least 10 states, the issue of who should be a beneficiary of a family support program was and is a problem. Specifically, many of the programs began with an orientation to either crisis intervention, avoidance of out-of-home placement, or to people with the most severe disabilities. As the experience of providers and families has grown, these distinctions become less and less useful. Our informants in many states saw a need for more expansive eligibility criteria but were also concerned that policy makers might mistake such moves as evidence of an endless demand for services.

3. *Statewide consistency.* Most states either have a regional system of services, depend on county agencies, or use local private providers. Ten state informants mentioned that there is a significant lack of uniformity in the administration or availability of family support in their state. A major source of tension for some families, this issue was particularly thorny in some states where family demand for more state level control placed the family support program in conflict with the way developmental disabilities services have traditionally been delivered in the state.

4. *Developing support services.* Four states indicated that while the state was proceeding to develop a mechanism for supporting families, the infrastructure needed to make this vision a reality was not in place. Basically, these states indicated that they had few community services that were not attached to a facility, whether a group home or institution. So while a family might be eligible for family supports, they may not be able to find a respite provider, an in-home behavior consultant, a parent support group, or any of the other services they needed.

5. *Accessing natural supports.* Two states highlighted the problem of trying to help families use generic community resources or the natural helping network of the families. Generally the people charged with this task came from a traditional background in developmental disabilities or social services and did not have a clue about how to go about realizing this goal.

6. *Developing a planning process.* Similarly, several states pointed out that once they bought into the strong value base attached to family support they were confronted with the need to develop a planning process congruent with this perspective. This was easier said than done, since this new approach required re-thinking of the relationship between family members and professionals and needed to give consideration to issues such as generic community resources.

7. *Staff development.* Two states specifically discussed the need to re-examine their general approach to staff development for people working within a family-centered system of supports. Numerous other states touched on this issue as they discussed the role of the case manager and highlighted how little a standard program of professional education prepared people for these new roles. In particular, they noted a need to help people understand the implications of integration and to use that as the guide in their professional practice.

8. *Interagency collaboration.* Another two states identified the need for a serious focus on interagency collaboration at the state, regional, and local levels as crucial to the success of a comprehensive approach to family support. As in the case of staff development, numerous other states touched on this same issue when they were asked to comment on the range of

family support efforts in their state. While some states seem aware of this need and have some sort of interagency information exchange, very few have taken even initial steps toward developing a cross-agency approach to supporting families.

Medicaid Policy

A major determinant of a state's overall commitment to supporting families can be seen in whether Medicaid policy has been used to finance family support. Table 3.2 indicates whether a state had at least one Medicaid waiver that provides some support for in-home care of children with a disability. But the presence of a single waiver does not demonstrate a family focus. The focus is in the degree to which a state has taken a family support perspective on use of Medicaid. In other words, has the state used a wide range of options available under regular Medicaid and through the various waiver options to make it easier for families of people with disabilities to obtain benefits under this program. Each state description provided an overview of the state policy. When these descriptions are reviewed, the five following policy directions emerge:

1. Twenty states indicated that Medicaid was not being used to provide family support nor was this policy under review.

2. In five states not using Medicaid to underwrite family supports, that policy was under review.

3. Four states reported that they were in the initial stages of implementing new options that allow Medicaid to cover some family supports.

4. Eleven states indicated that they regard Medicaid as one mechanism for supporting families, and they make relatively limited use of it to support activities such as respite or case management.

5. Ten states saw Medicaid as a major source of supports to families and were making or planning to make extensive use of it to achieve that goal.

Related Efforts

To gain a sense of the degree to which family support extended beyond the mental retardation/developmental disabilities agency and the developmental disabilities council, we asked our informants to tell us about other family support efforts in their state. In general, the information that emerged was of relatively limited utility. Most informants had little knowledge of family supports in other parts of state government, and many of the responses amounted to little more than "They should be doing something in the . . . department" or "I think I heard that . . . had a program." The one related effort that most informants knew of was the early intervention program.

On average, our state informants were able to identify two related family support efforts. The range was from no useful information in seven states to substantial knowledge about five family supports efforts in Minnesota. After early intervention, the most frequently identified family support initiatives were in the state's health department, specifically the maternal and child health division and the services to children with disabilities under Title V. Nineteen of our informants were aware of an interest in issues related to family support in the state mental health agency. Other departments that were identified as having family support efforts were children and youth, social or human services, and rehabilitation. Nine states indicated that private groups in their state were the primary impetus for family support. As we noted earlier, the findings in this area are probably more indicative of the need for increased interagency communication and collaboration on family supports than they are a measure of what is actually occurring in each state.

Lessons Learned

The final two sections of findings summarize our informants' opinions of the most valuable lessons states have learned about developing support for families and what they see as future directions. The major lessons highlighted by our informants centered on issues related to the initial design and development of a family support program. In particular, they emphasized the following:

1. There is a need to listen to parents at all stages in designing and developing family support efforts.
2. Those involved in developing a system of family supports need to be politically realistic and savvy.
3. A number of practical issues need to be addressed:
 • Family support efforts must remain flexible and evaluations should be conducted periodically to ensure ongoing responsiveness.
 • Given the newness of the concept, it is useful to start family support programs as demonstrations in order to persuade policy makers regarding the effectiveness of family support.
 • Family support programs need staff who are well trained in a family-centered approach to services.
 • People involved in providing family support have to learn to coordinate all the various systems that impinge on a family's life.

Family support providers need to learn about the natural resources and community supports that can be tapped for families.

4. A permanent system of family supports should be underpinned by a parent-run, grass roots political organization with specific goals such as the passage of legislation.

5. It is important for family support efforts to establish clear guidelines and principles at the beginning.

6. The focus on parent control must be firmly ingrained from the outset.

7. Providers should not expect families to believe from the outset that family support services will actually empower them and be family-centered—they will believe it when the programs live up to their rhetoric.

Future Direction

When asked to project what the future holds for family supports in their states, our informants were very positive. They all saw growth in some form or another. Growth was projected in seven areas:

1. *Family support will become the centerpiece of our system of services.* In 12 states, the informants saw family support as defining the future of all services for people with disabilities. They spoke of it as providing the basis for reordering the state budget for services or converting the old system of services to one that focuses on families and individuals.

2. *Our state will develop a system of family supports.* In all of the states without a family support effort and in one state with a very small pilot project (10 states total), the informants indicated that efforts were underway to establish family support as something with its own unique identity.

3. *We are developing an awareness of "family support" among families, the public, and policy makers.* In 9 states that had either a pilot or a very small program, the informants saw the next step as a public relations effort to increase awareness about this new thing called "family support."

4. *The state will expand the range of services available to families.* Informants in 8 states felt that the major issue in the area of family support was the lack of sufficient services either throughout the state or in selected regions. Hence they saw the immediate future involving growth in the range of services that they called family support.

5. *We will develop the day-to-day expertise needed to support families.* Five state informants expressed some variant of the position that "We've got the values, principles, and ideology. In the immediate future we have got to develop the expertise to make all of this a reality."

6. *We will make family supports a permanent part of what we do in this state.* In 5 of the states with pilot projects, the future revolved around an effort to translate the experience of the pilot into a permanent state program.

7. *We will increase the level of family control.* Finally, in 3 states with relatively well developed systems of supports, the informants felt that their

systems were overly controlled by professionals and the future would see an increase in family control.

DISCUSSION

At this admittedly early stage in their development, supports for families of people with disabilities are at a crucial juncture. Almost every state has come to the conclusion that family support is something that it should do, but what remains undecided in most states is the direction that these efforts will take. In general, the efforts we found were small-scale and very new. Nationally, and in most individual states, the actual fiscal commitment to family support is a minute portion of the total budget for developmental disabilities services—facility-based programs continue to absorb the bulk of the resources. To this point, most family support has been "sold" to policy makers based almost exclusively on a rationale of cost effectiveness. This is a crisis intervention perspective that sees the public sector providing just enough assistance to maintain the family and avoid the demand for an expensive out of the home placement. Only in the last year or two have a few states begun to confront the basic message of family support: *It is about the ultimate reconfiguration of developmental disabilities services away from facility-based models to a true community system.*

As we noted in the introduction, the last decade has seen most states make the decision to get out of the business of running large congregate care institutions. Our reading of the direction in family supports leads us to conclude that within the next decade each state will confront another fundamental decision about its policy direction. In its most concise form, the question confronting policy makers is "Will we continue with business as usual, placing our primary emphasis on funding programs and facilities and providing minimal support to families and adults with disabilities who live outside our facilities, or will we shift to a truly individually driven system in which we fund the unique constellation of services and supports that each person needs?"

A few states that have recently passed family support legislation have clearly set a course in the direction of this fundamental reconfiguration of services. Another small core of states that have some history in providing comprehensive family support are presently grappling with the challenge of expanding their efforts to reach out to a broader range of families and the implications that this model of support has for the other components in their system of services. Some larger states with expansive community services that are configured around a system of facilities are only beginning to realize the long-term implications of family support for this system and are in the process of making decisions that will determine whether family support is an adjunct to this existing system or the hallmark of a fundamental reordering. Finally, the majority of states are only starting to explore family support and the support of individuals and do not as yet fully appreciate the implications of making a full commitment to supporting families.

In conclusion, a final point needs to be made regarding this and any subsequent efforts to describe state family support practices. There are likely to be significant differences between the ideal of family support as it emerges from interviews with policy makers and providers or review of state legislation, regulations, or other documents and the reality of families' experience. As an example, we can consider respite nominally the most readily available family support. Based on the figures presented in this report, it would seem that most families that have a child with a developmental disability should be able to obtain some level of publicly supported respite. However, a recent survey of parents' experiences with respite (Knoll & Bedford, 1989) found that although respite appears to be widely available, in many cases this service is not truly accessible to families. This suggests that any future efforts to assess state efforts in the area of family supports should supplement any survey of administrators and policy makers with an evaluation by consumers in an effort to determine the degree to which the ideals of family support are truly being realized.

REFERENCES

Administration on Developmental Disabilities. (1988). *Special Projects Program: Abstracts of funded programs for fiscal year 1985–87*. Washington, DC: Author.
Agosta, J. M., & Bradley, V. J. (Eds.). (1985). *Family care for persons with developmental disabilities: A growing commitment*. Cambridge, MA: Human Services Research Institute.
Bates, M. V. (1985). *State family support/cash subsidy programs*. Madison, WI: Council on Developmental Disabilities.
Bird, W. (1984). *A survey of family support programs in seventeen states*. Albany: New York State Office of Mental Retardation and Developmental Disabilities.
Braddock, D., Hemp, R., Fujiura, G., Bachelder, L., & Mitchell, D. (1990). *The state of the states in developmental disabilities*. Baltimore: Brookes.
Bronheim, S., Cohen, P. D., & Magrab, P. (1985). *Evaluating community collaboration: A guide to self-study*. Washington, DC: Georgetown University, Child Developmental Center.
Center on Human Policy. (1987). *A statement in support of families and their children*. Syracuse, NY: Author.
Cohen, S., Agosta, J., Cohen, J., & Warren, R. (1989). Supporting the families of children with severe disabilities. *The Journal of the Association for Persons with Severe Handicaps, 14*, 155–162.
Dunst, C. J., Trivette, C. M., & Deal, A. G. (1988). *Enabling and empowering families: Principles and guidelines for practice*. Cambridge, MA: Brookline Books.
Ellison, M. L., Bradley, V. J., Knoll, J., & Moore, K. (1989). *Financing options for home care for children with chronic illness and severe disability: Technical assistance manual*. Cambridge, MA: Human Services Research Institute.
Gallagher, J. J., & Vietze, P. M. (1986). *Families of handicapped persons: Research, programs, and policy issues*. Baltimore: Brookes.
Gaylord, C. L., & Leonard, A. M. (1988). *Health care coverage for a child with a chronic illness or disability*. Madison, WI: Center for Public Representation.

Goldfarb, L. A., Botherson, M. J., Summers, J. A., & Turnbull, A. P. (1986). *Meeting the challenge of disability or chronic illness: A family guide.* Baltimore: Brookes.
Hazel, R., Barber, P. A., Roberts, S., Behr, S. K., Helmstetter, E., & Guess, D. (1988). *A community approach to an integrated system for children with special needs.* Baltimore: Brookes.
Jones, M. (1985). *Home care for the chronically mentally ill or disabled child: A manual and source book for parents and professionals.* New York: Harper and Row.
Kaufman, J., & Lichtenstein, K. A. (1986). *The family as care manager: Home care coordination for the medically fragile child.* Washington, DC: Georgetown University, Child Development Center.
Knoll, J. A., & Bedford, S. (1989). *Becoming informed consumers: A national survey of parents' experience with respite services.* Cambridge, MA: Human Services Research Institute.
Koop, C. E. (1987). *Surgeon General's report: Children with special health care needs.* Rockville, MD: U.S. Department of Health and Human Services, Public Health Service.
Maternal and Child Health. (1988). *Family-centered care.* Rockville, MD: U.S. Department of Health and Human Services, Public Health Service, Division of Maternal and Child Health.
Nelkin, V. (1987). *Family-centered health care for medically fragile children: Principles and practices.* Washington, DC: Georgetown University, Child Development Center.
Shaffer, H., & Cross, J. (1989). *Call to the field: Research on families and disability, 1988–1989.* Lawrence: University of Kansas, Beach Center on Families and Disability.
Singer, G. H. S., & Irvin, L. (1989). *Support for caregiving families: Enabling positive adaptation to disability.* Baltimore: Brookes.
Skarnulis, E. (1979). Support, not supplant, the natural home: Serving handicapped children and adults. In S. Maybanks & M. Bryce (Eds.), *Home-based services for children and families* (pp. 64–76). Springfield, IL: Charles C Thomas.
Taylor, S. J., Lakin K. C., & Hill, B. K. (1989). Permanency planning for children and youth: Out-of-home placement decisions. *Exceptional Children, 55,* 541–549.
United Cerebral Palsy Associations. (1987). *Policy on family support for children with disabilities.* Washington, DC: United Cerebral Palsy Associations, Community Services Division.

Chapter 4

John Agosta

Evaluating Family Support Services
Two Quantitative Case Studies

INTRODUCTION

As noted in the previous chapter on state family support programs across the nation, such services are expanding rapidly. The somewhat radical departure that family support programs have taken from the conventional approach to services raises questions regarding how they can best be administered and whether they in fact are making a difference in the lives of families. Singer and Irvin (1989) present a succinct description of the various evaluation strategies that may be applied to family support programs and concludes that the issues are so numerous and the dimensions of success so complex that multiple means of evaluation must be pursued. They also present a matrix for evaluating programs that includes both formative and summative evaluation and takes into account the service context, program input, processes, and products. Given this design, many variables can be explored including those keyed to the child, the family, the service program, and the overall system of services.

For our purposes, we were specifically interested in whether the families who participate in family support programs are better off as a result. This chapter presents information on the outcomes of family support drawn from the findings of quantitative studies of family support programs in Iowa and Illinois. In Iowa, a state sponsored program provided families with a monthly cash subsidy of about $261; no other support services were offered. In Illinois the state's Planning Council on Developmental Disabilities sponsored four pilot programs to test various means of supporting families. All of these pilots utilized a combination of support services and cash assistance.

Acknowledgment. Preparation of this chapter was supported with funds from the Iowa and Illinois Planning Councils on Developmental Disabilities. All opinions expressed herein are solely those of the author and do not reflect the position or policy of either of the two Planning Councils.

THE IOWA FAMILY SUPPORT SUBSIDY PROGRAM

In 1988, the Iowa Legislature established a family support subsidy program to assist families in Iowa to "stay together and to reduce the number of placements in public or private facilities by defraying some of the special costs of caring for a child who requires certain special education services" (Iowa Legislative Statute, 1988, 225C.36). At first, eligibility was restricted to families who (a) were providing care at home to a child up to the age of 18 years who was classified within the special education system as having a "severe" disability, (b) indicated that they were seeking an out-of-home placement for their child, and (c) had an annual taxable income of $40,000 or less.[1]

The Family Support Subsidy law authorizes Iowa's Department of Human Services (DHS) to provide monthly payments (set in 1991 at $261 per month) directly to eligible families. The amount is keyed to the federal Supplemental Security Income (SSI) program and provides an amount equivalent to the monthly SSI payment of an adult living in the home of another, minus an allowance subtracted by the state for room and board.

The program was implemented on December 16, 1988, and the first families began receiving payments in January 1989. During the first fiscal year, 109 applications were received and 54 children in 53 families received monthly subsidy payments. Forty-eight families remained on the waiting list at the end of the first fiscal year (seven applicants were deemed ineligible). Additional funds were allocated after the first year, and at the time this evaluation was conducted, about 140 families were receiving subsidy payments. In January 1991, 175 families were receiving the subsidy, while the waiting list had grown to 436 families.

In addition to establishing administrative guidelines, Iowa's family support legislation directed that an evaluation of the subsidy program be undertaken. During the program's first year, DHS completed the mandated evaluation (Cunningham, 1989). For its second year of operation, however, the legislature directed that the Iowa Governor's Planning Council for Developmental Disabilities (PCDD) complete the evaluation required of DHS, and they in turn contracted with the Human Services Research Institute to carry out the analysis (see Agosta, Deatherage, Keating, Bradley, & Knoll, 1990). Results stemming from this second year evaluation are reported here.

---

[1]During the program's first year, families complained about (a) the need to have a special education "weight" of 2.2 or 3.6 in order to qualify for the program and (b) criteria that required families to indicate that they had considered out-of-home placement for their child. In response, both criteria were eliminated.

For the purpose of this evaluation, two questions were asked: Did the family support subsidy program accomplish its goals? What further issues were raised during the course of the evaluation of the subsidy program?

Evaluation Methods

Design of the Survey Form

A survey form was designed to gather information on those families receiving the subsidy, their family members, and their experiences with the program. The form covered six primary areas of inquiry, included 34 questions, and was designed to take approximately 20 to 30 minutes to complete.[2] Descriptions of the six domains and the types of questions included follow:

- *Family information*: Nine questions about the characteristics of the caregiving families (e.g., county of residence, household composition, care responsibilities, family income, opportunity costs).
- *Information on the family member with a disability*: Eight questions about the family member with a disability (e.g., age, sex, and level of assistance required).
- *Family needs profile*: A single question composed of 42 Likert-scaled items designed to check the level of family need in a variety of areas. The scale required respondents to circle a number from 1 (low) to 5 (high) that best described the level of need.
- *Future placement plans*: Three questions requesting information on any plans for residential placement.
- *Supports received by the family*: Three questions about the family's sources of support, including government benefits and informal supports, and a fourth asking what the family had purchased with their subsidy funds.
- *Family opinion*: This section included nine questions designed to solicit respondents' opinions about their experiences with the subsidy program, including the impact of the program on their lives and their satisfaction with the program. It also included several open-ended questions.

Distribution of the Survey Forms

This study surveyed 140 families who had been receiving the subsidy for the majority of the fiscal year prior to June 1990. Survey packets were provided to the Iowa Planning Council and DHS staff, who distributed them to the families. Each packet included a letter from a DHS administrator

---

[2] A copy of the Iowa Cash Subsidy Survey Form can be obtained through the Human Services Research Institute at 2336 Massachusetts Avenue, Cambridge, MA 02140.

explaining the evaluation, the survey form, and a pre-stamped and addressed envelope in which to return the completed questionnaire to the evaluation team. To track responses, each packet and survey form was given a number (1–140). DHS staff in Iowa assigned a number to each family, but the evaluation team was not given any family's name.

Compilation and Analysis of the Data

Each of the returned forms was precoded to track return patterns and to simplify the data compilation process. Returned questionnaires were first screened to assess whether the information could be used. Completed survey forms were to be removed from further consideration if numerous questions were left unanswered or responses could not be understood or if the family did not participate in the subsidy program. In fact, no survey forms were eliminated from subsequent analyses, and the number of families returning survey forms totaled 120, a response rate of 85.7%.

Following initial review, data were entered into a specially designed microcomputer data base and prepared for analysis through extensive error checks. A specialized data entry program was used to ensure maximum accuracy and efficiency by trained data entry personnel. Once the data were entered, SPSS PC+ statistics software was used in subsequent analyses.

Survey Results

A selection of responses to the open-ended questions appears below; frequency counts for many of the survey items and displays of several scale scores that were computed based on initial frequencies are presented in the following summary analysis. In 105 of the 120 cases (88%), the primary respondent was the family member's mother, with other respondents distributed among several other family members.

Responses to Open-Ended Questions

A final section of the survey form invited respondents to write in their responses to several open-ended questions. What follows is a sampling of the responses offered.

Overall feelings about the subsidy program:

> "This was the first relief that came to us. We were desperate when that first check came—we were elated and filled with humility and gratitude. . . Our government cares more than friends, family and even churches!! We would never have kept on 'keeping on' without it."

On lack of program publicity:

"If a friend hadn't happened to tell me about it, I wouldn't have known the Family Subsidy Program existed."

"It seemed to be a well-kept secret. We found out about the program accidently and just barely got our application in on time. There are a lot more families in the state that could use this help!"

On the amount of the subsidy:

"$257 makes a difference in our life—but it doesn't come close to meeting the costs of our child's special needs."

"I also think the income levels could be raised even higher so that more middle income families could benefit from this program. It takes a lot of money to properly care for a child with severe physical disabilities; much, much more so than for a nondisabled child, and very few families have the extra income needed."

"My health insurance policy is $799.30 a month."

Concern for future program instability:

"I am always worried that we'll somehow lose this privilege and we need it so badly."

"We are always uncertain if funding will be continued. Also there are so many more families who could truly benefit. There's such a need that is not being met."

On ending program eligibility at age 18:

"I least appreciate the fact that it is based on our income and that it ends when our daughter is 18—that is when we'll really need services and assistance."

"If these programs are designed to keep us from placing our child in an institution then why do they end at age 18? SSI does not begin to cover expenses incurred for services."

On other needs the subsidy does not address:

"I only wish there was more help in our county for handicapped persons, such as someone to care so I could have a break for an afternoon or evening."

"I can't get anyone out to my home from Respite Care in evenings."

"I would like to see a program that would help make your home handicap accessible. I am in the process of trying to find another place to live because of this reason. I really can't afford to move."

On the adequacy of the program:

"The program is so nice for families with kids with disabilities that there should be more funding. Even though more funding and more families have been added, with the waiting list as there is, there are still plenty of families that also fall between the cracks that would benefit from this program."

"The subsidy is great for regular use, but in an emergency it wouldn't go very far. Nursing and home health care can be expensive."

Summary Analysis of Survey Findings

The Family Member with A Disability

The majority of family members were nine years old or younger (62%), but not all ages under nine were equally represented. If fact, the birth-to-three group had the fewest members (7.5%) among subsidy recipients. As noted in the earlier DHS evaluation (Cunningham, 1989), the original eligibility requirement of a special education weighting essentially excluded children under age 3 because they could not be assigned a score. Thirty percent of recipients were between ages 10 and 15; slightly more than half were boys (52%).

When evaluating the impact of their child's disabilities (Table 4.1), respondents reported "a lot" of need for assistance in completing daily activities (67%), communicating with others (71%), and in the area of physical mobility (59%). In contrast, while several persons were judged to require specialized medical attention (13% daily and 7% weekly), the majority did not. Of particular interest are the responses concerning challenging behavior. For 55%, this is either never an issue or occurs less than monthly,

TABLE 4.1

Impact of the Disability on the Child with the Disability

AREA OF PERFORMANCE AFFECTED	NONE	A LITTLE	SOME	A LOT
Mental/intellectual development[b]	0	4	27	88
Physical mobility[c]	14	16	19	69
Communication with others	5	10	20	85
Assistance needed in daily activities	7	15	18	80
	<MONTHLY	MONTHLY	WEEKLY	DAILY
Specialized medical attention[d]	54	40	8	15
Challenging behavior[d]	65	7	9	37

[a] Survey question: "How much/how often does the disability affect performance?" [b] 1 missing response. [c] 2 missing responses. [d] 3 missing responses.

but for 31%, it is a daily problem. Overall, these data suggest that as a whole, the program is serving families with children who have severe disabilities and major support needs.

Family Composition and Caregiving

The majority of family respondents (53%) lived within households of four persons or less. For 63%, the child's mother was the primary caregiver, while in 33% the mother and father had equal responsibility. Fourteen percent were single parent families. A relatively large percentage of families (18%) included others in the home with significant mental, health, or emotional problems.

In many instances, family members reported that they either limited their job choice (68%), did not look for a job (50%), or gave up a job (41%) due to the demands of providing care at home. Although no data are available for a comparable group of Iowan families who do not include a family member with a disability, these statistics represent a very high cost in lost income to families and lost tax revenues to the state. Sixteen percent of families changed jobs for better medical benefits, and 14% lost health insurance coverage for reasons related to their family member.

Over half (56%) said they lived where they did because of their child's disability for one of several reasons: to be near services, in order not to lose services, because of architectural needs, or not moving to a better home because of the cost of care. In some cases families felt they had to move because their child's disability disturbed the landlord or neighbors. Nearly half (48%) of the families receiving the subsidy earned less than $20,000 per year, with 22% earning under $10,000.

Family Needs, Supports and Placement Plans

Family needs were assessed over 42 topic areas (see Table 4.2). A discussion of the findings follows:

- Family needs cannot be confined to a "short list." Rather, each family is unique and may have many far ranging needs, or just a few. *The number of needs listed by a family, however, should not be confused with the magnitude of any single need or its impact on the family.*
- When viewed in the aggregate, the frequency distributions for most items suggest that families typically do not indicate a high need and in many instances indicate "no need." This point is illustrated by Figure 4.1, given a display of total family needs as an overall scale score. The distribution of scores suggests that few families have high needs in most areas, but that most seem to have needs in relatively few of the areas listed.
- For a number of the areas assessed, such as getting special equipment, adapting the house, or getting an appropriate school program, the

TABLE 4.2
Family Needs Profile

TYPE OF NEED	NOT A NEED	SOME	VERY HIGH NEED	MISSING
Having enough money for the basics our family needs or to pay bills	17	43	22	22	2
Affording a phone	74	15	22	3	6	0
Getting clothing for all family members	38	18	33	14	15	2
Getting information about our child's needs and how to meet them	30	20	36	15	19	0
Getting information on our child's legal rights	34	25	23	22	16	0
Getting financial assistance from government agencies	23	21	27	18	31	0
Finding ways to help our child become more independent in caring for his or her own needs	33	18	22	18	28	1
Fixing our home to make it easier for our child to get around	49	17	18	7	28	1
Fixing our home to make it safer for our child	52	19	20	8	20	1
Transporting our child around town	43	23	16	17	21	0
Getting special travel equipment (lifts, car seats, etc.)	58	14	8	10	29	1
Getting special equipment for our child (wheelchair, language board, etc.)	46	12	15	16	30	1
Providing a special diet or clothing for our child	49	25	18	12	15	1
Getting our child into school or into a day program	74	12	13	6	15	0
Getting a program that meets our child's needs once in school	41	20	19	10	30	0
Finding enough opportunities for our child to recreate or have fun away from home	18	12	26	23	40	1
Finding enough opportunities for our child to make friends with persons who do not have a disability	34	18	23	16	29	0
Getting special therapies for our child (speech, physical, occupational)	34	18	26	12	29	1
Getting counselling for our child	82	17	12	1	6	2
Getting medical and dental care for our child	54	18	22	12	13	1

Finding trained medical professionals who will come to our home to provide care (nurses, home health care)	62	17	11	6	2
Getting adequate health insurance for our child	61	7	12	10	1
Getting someone to come into our house and provide care to our child while I am away for short periods of time	32	13	24	14	0
Getting someone to come into our house and provide care to our child while I am away for long periods of time (evening, weekends, vacation)	23	11	21	18	0
Getting care for our child during work hours (day care)	61	12	13	11	0
Finding a place away from home where our child can go when I need a break	27	15	19	12	0
Finding someone to care for our child in an emergency	26	11	21	18	0
Planning for the future service needs of our child	12	10	27	18	0
Planning for what will happen when we can no longer care for our child	19	7	18	22	1
Planning for the future financial security of our child	8	7	13	25	0
Finding ways to cope with the stress related to my providing care to our child	11	16	31	23	1
Explaining our child's disability to others	39	24	26	15	1
Learning how to cope with family problems	25	28	24	22	0
Managing a family budget	34	27	30	13	1
Having someone to talk to (family members, friends)	46	20	24	11	0
Finding enough time for myself	14	13	29	20	2
Finding enough time for other family members	18	16	26	26	0
Finding time to complete household chores and routines	24	17	28	25	0
Finding time to socialize with friends	17	16	21	29	2
Vacationing or having fun as a family	14	12	18	20	0
Participating in support groups for parents or other family members	36	16	26	19	2
Getting counselling for parents or other family members	51	26	18	8	0

[a] Survey question: "To what extent does your family have a need NOW for help or assistance?"

TOTAL FAMILY NEED SCORES

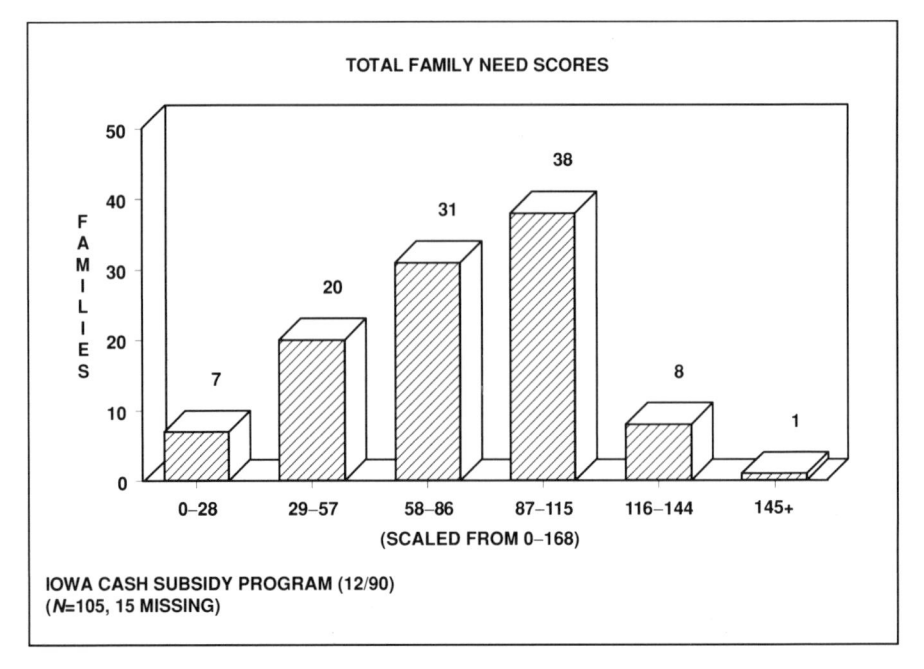

Range (Scaled from 0–168)	Families
0–28	7
29–57	20
58–86	31
87–115	38
116–144	8
145+	1

IOWA CASH SUBSIDY PROGRAM (12/90)
(*N*=105, 15 MISSING)

FIGURE 4.1: This scale on *total family needs* was developed based on the responses to the questions displayed in Table 4.2. To create the scale, responses to the 42 need areas were first recoded from 0–4. Second, for each respondent, the responses across all 42 areas were summed to yield a score that could range from 0–168 (4×42). The higher the score, the greater is the overall level of family need. Figure 4.1 displays the scale scores. The *internal consistency* (measured by the Cronbach alpha statistic) for the 42-item scale was computed at .896.

frequency distributions suggest that needs are either high or low, with little middle ground. Different disabilities may create different patterns of need; a careful analysis of data should enable the program to predict and plan for needs based on eligibility guidelines.

At first glance it may be surprising that some families still indicate areas of "very high need" after having been enrolled for at least one year at the time of the survey. But many of these areas are beyond the scope of a family support program that is limited to a subsidy payment. Some are service-related, such as getting respite care for short (30%) or long (39%) periods, getting special equipment (25%), or getting special therapies (24%). In some cases, particularly in rural areas, services are not widely available, even when a family has funds to purchase them. A family support program limited to a subsidy does not include resources for training service providers, nor does it directly offer information and referral.

Other high need areas not directly addressed by a subsidy program include vacationing as a family (47%), finding opportunities for the child to recreate or have fun away from home (34%), or finding opportunities for the child to make friends (24%). Another major issue that families in Iowa confront, getting health insurance (24%), is also not addressed by a subsidy program alone.

- The findings suggest that families receive help from a variety of sources, but most of the help comes from the immediate family (i.e., spouse or other children) or close, extended family (e.g., grandparents). Other potential sources of support (e.g., churches, neighbors) are not often utilized. The subsidy program in Iowa presently does not provide assistance to families in identifying and acquiring help.
- Interestingly, 41 families (34%) indicated a high need for special therapies for their child (speech, physical or occupational). Thirty of these 41 families cared for children who were aged five years or more. As these children all received school services, one is left to wonder why special education services were not providing these therapies as part of the children's Individual Education Plans. As a consequence, 8 of the 41 families used their subsidy dollars to obtain therapy services.
- The initial eligibility requirements of Iowa's Family Support Subsidy legislation included a provision that either the child be a resident of an out-of-home residential program with a discharge plan to return home within 60 days, or that "placement for the child has been considered in a state hospital-school, a community-based intermediate care facility for persons with mental retardation or developmental disabilities, a child foster family or group home, or a state mental health institute." (The law was subsequently revised to delete any need for considering an out-of-home placement.)

Three respondents said they were planning to bring their child home at the time they applied to the program, and four reported they had actually brought their child home as a result of receiving the subsidy. Only 49 families (41%) indicated they were considering out-of-home placement at the time they applied for the subsidy.

The fact that fewer than half of the respondents report now that their family actually met one of the eligibility requirements reveals the inherent difficulty in restricting family support only to those who say they are willing to give up their child. If we are serious when we say that family support is "whatever it takes" to support families in caring for their child with a disability at home, we can understand that parents may feel compelled to do "whatever it takes" to obtain services their child desperately needs. "Considering" placing a child out of the home is an ambiguous term and may be interpreted as merely thinking of the possibility. Of the 49 who

TABLE 4.3

Items Purchased by Families with the Subsidy

SERVICE/ITEM PURCHASED[a]	FREQUENCY OF PURCHASE
Sitter for child	83
Educational aids or toys for child	79
Transportation	77
Medical expenses and health-related items	75
Recreation	65
Respite care for child	54
Diapers	48
Adaptive equipment	47
Special foods	42
Home renovation	29
Insurance	22
Camp	18
Parent training	15
Individual or family counselling	14
Clothing	14
Therapy (physical, occupational, or speech)	11
Household expenses (to pay bills)	8
Homemaker services	6
Household items (miscellaneous household expenses)	3
Home nursing care	1

[a]Survey question: "Listed below are some services and items which may help families care for the special needs of their child with disabilities. Please indicate which of them your family has purchased with your family support subsidy."

said they had considered out-of-home placement, 40 (82%) reported they had changed their minds as a result of receiving the subsidy and were no longer considering (or planning) placing their child. Four of those families had actually withdrawn their applications, and six were no longer looking for an appropriate placement.

- The most popular use of the cash offered families was to purchase sitter services for their child. But, as illustrated by Table 4.3, families used the money to purchase a variety of goods and services.
- Families indicated that they received support from multiple sources, both from the public sector and from other informal and private sources (Table 4.4).
- Ninety-six percent of the 49 families who were considering placement reported that the subsidy program had influenced their decision to have their child continue to live at home. The majority (53%) indicated the subsidy had greatly influenced their decision, an additional 10% indicated that it had influenced them somewhat, while 32% said it had slightly influenced their decision. These findings are consistent with, but even stronger than, those of the DHS evaluation of August 1989 (Cunningham, 1989).

TABLE 4.4

Other Sources of Help

SOURCE OF HELP[a]	n
Family members	78
Professional helpers	63
Relatives outside the home	55
Friends	48
Other parents of children with disabilities	41
Church members	20
Neighbors	18
Other	3

[a] Survey question: "Whom do you consider a significant help to you and your family in meeting the challenges you face because of your child's disability?" Respondents were given the option of indicating more than one response.

From the program's start in 1988 through 1990, only two children were placed out of home, one in August 1989 and the other in July 1990. Four families stopped receiving the subsidy when their children passed age 18. Another family was terminated from the program when their child died, and another was terminated for unknown reasons.

Yet these data may be confounded by the fact that the original program was limited to families who were considering out-of-home placement. If some applicants made this stipulation only to become eligible for the program, they may have felt the need to be consistent on the survey questions, or their responses may have been closer to their real intent to maintain the child at home. Either way, the data must be interpreted with caution.

Family Opinion

Families answered 9 items related to the impact of the program on family life using a 5-point scale where 1 = not at all and 5 = a great deal, as shown by Table 4.5. On 7 of 9 items, over half of the respondents selected 4 or 5. Overall, the results show that families in the program felt that it had a very positive impact on many aspects of their lives. The items that received the strongest positive scores were "eased financial worries because of child," "improved family's life overall," and "helped family do more together." Each of these items can clearly be related to the presence of additional income in the family. Areas with the lowest impact scores were in helping to get to know persons outside the family in the community and in easing worries about the future well-being of the child. These results are not surprising given the one-dimensional character of the family support subsidy, which does not presently assist families with integration or future planning strategies.

TABLE 4.5
Impact of the Program on Family Life

TYPE OF IMPACT	NOT AT ALL		SOME		A GREAT DEAL
Improved your family's life overall	1	5	34	34	46
Improved your ability to care for your child	2	12	34	34	38
Helped your family to do more together	8	8	25	34	45
Helped your family be more like other families	13	21	30	24	32
Eased your financial worries because of your child[b]	2	7	29	31	50
Eased your worries about the future well-being of your child	21	23	32	22	22
Reduced the stress in your family's life	7	13	48	25	27
Helped you do things that you were unable to do before[b]	8	6	40	27	38
Helped you to get to know other persons in your community outside your family	44	26	34	7	9

Degree of Impact[a]

[a] Survey question: "Regarding the program's impact on your family, circle the number that best describes the program's effect." [b] 1 missing response.

The large majority of families indicated a great deal of satisfaction over how the program was administered (Table 4.6). Families were particularly satisfied with the way they were treated by program staff, with about 83% indicating a great deal of satisfaction (4 or 5 using a scale similar to that described above). Eighty percent were greatly satisfied with what the program had helped them achieve so far. The lowest satisfaction was expressed with the timeliness of the subsidy payments (61%) and the information

TABLE 4.6
Satisfaction with the Program by Item

ASPECT OF PROGRAM	NOT AT ALL		SOME		A GREAT DEAL
The amount of subsidy in helping you take care of your family's special needs[b]	2	6	29	38	44
The application procedure[b]	3	5	24	36	51
The timeliness of subsidy payments	2	10	35	71	2
The information you have received about the program[b]	6	8	27	32	46
The way you have been treated by persons involved with the program[b]	1	4	15	32	67
What the program has helped you achieve so far[c]	0	0	23	42	52

Degree of Satisfaction[a]

[a] Survey question: "Describe how satisfied you are with the family support program. How satisfied are you with . . .?" [b] 1 missing response. [c] 3 missing responses.

IMPACT ON FAMILY LIFE

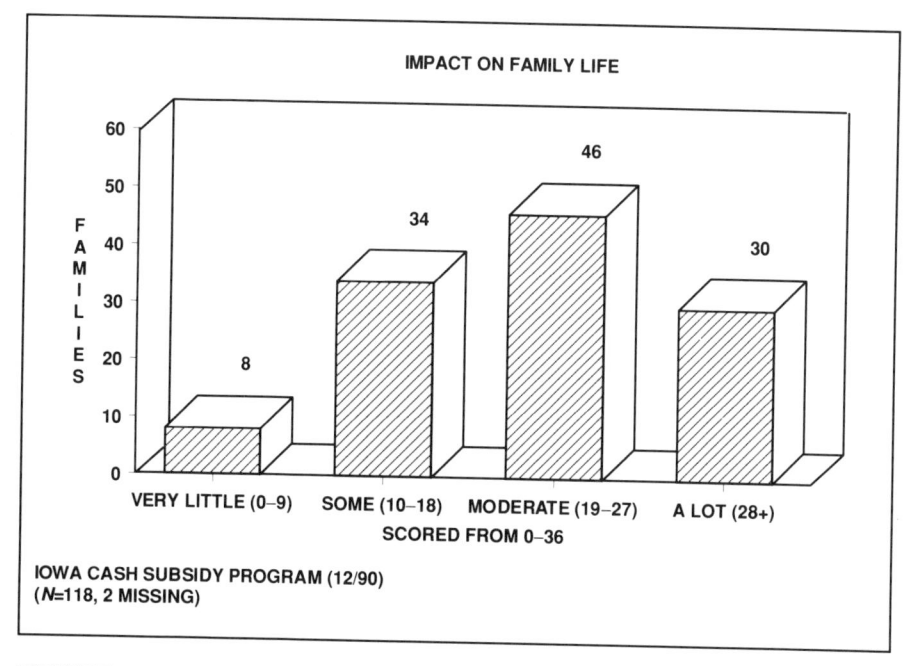

(Bar chart showing FAMILIES on y-axis from 0 to 60)
- VERY LITTLE (0-9): 8
- SOME (10-18): 34
- MODERATE (19-27): 46
- A LOT (28+): 30

SCORED FROM 0-36

IOWA CASH SUBSIDY PROGRAM (12/90)
(N=118, 2 MISSING)

FIGURE 4.2: This scale on *total family impact* was developed based on the responses to the questions displayed in Table 4.5. To create the scale, responses were recoded from 0–4 and then summed to yield a score that could from 0–36 (4×9). The higher the score, the greater the family impact. Figure 4.2 displays the scale scores. The *internal consistency* (measured by the Cronbach alpha statistic) for the 9-item scale was computed at .917.

received about the program (66%). Note that even areas of lowest satisfaction scored well over 50%.

Scale scores for impact on family life (Figure 4.2) were either moderate or high for 64% of the sample, indicating that a significant proportion of families (about a third) felt that the program had only a modest influence on their lives. This is not surprising given that family circumstances and needs may well demand a more varied support network than cash alone can provide. Families, however, appreciated the help and, as depicted by Figure 4.3, they expressed great overall satisfaction with the program.

Unlike many other states, Iowa's Family Support Subsidy Program did not include "family consultants" to assist families. Fifty-seven percent of the respondents said they would like someone to be available to help them use the subsidy program, primarily to assist in locating and obtaining services and resources. This is consistent with the results reported that

SATISFACTION WITH THE PROGRAM

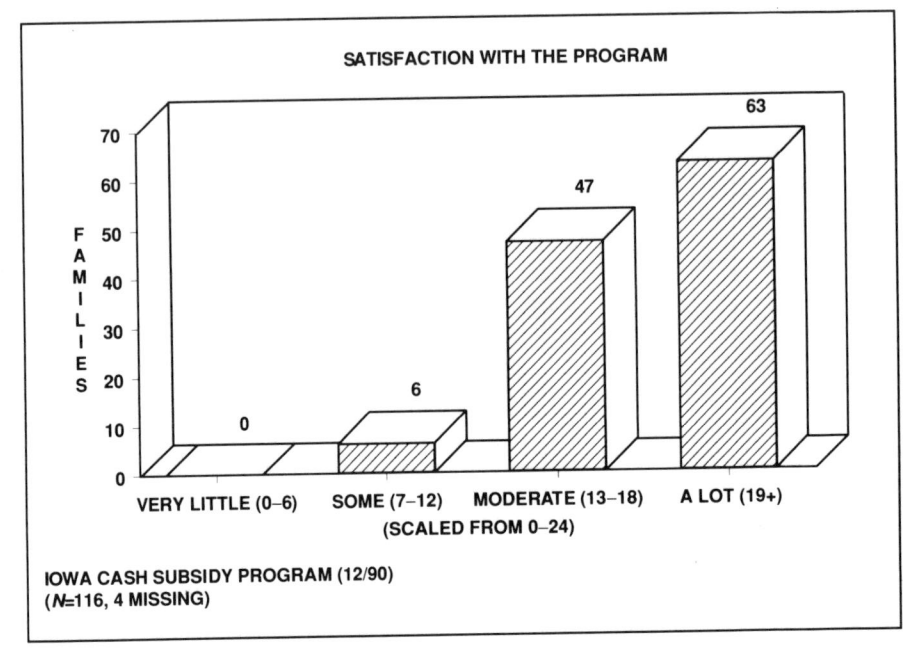

Bar chart showing FAMILIES by satisfaction category (scaled from 0–24):
- VERY LITTLE (0–6): 0
- SOME (7–12): 6
- MODERATE (13–18): 47
- A LOT (19+): 63

IOWA CASH SUBSIDY PROGRAM (12/90)
(N=116, 4 MISSING)

FIGURE 4.3: This scale on *family satisfaction* is based on the responses given to the questions displayed in Table 4.6. To create the scale, responses were recoded from 0–4 and summed to yield a score that could range from 0–24 (4×6). The higher the score, the greater the satisfaction. Figure 4.3 displays the scale scores. The *internal consistency* (measured by the Cronbach alpha statistic) for the 6-item scale was computed at .793.

indicate a residual need for services and interventions not part of the subsidy program as presently configured.

Regarding the amount of control felt by families over the services received, survey findings suggest that respondents felt a greater sense of control within the subsidy program than within other services (Table 4.7).

Discussion Relevant to the Two Evaluation Questions

Question 1: Did the family support subsidy program accomplish its goals?

The initial goals of the program as stated within the enacting legislation were to assist families in Iowa to "stay together and to reduce the number of placements in public or private facilities by defraying some of the special costs of caring for a child who requires certain special education services." In July 1990 these goals were modified to eliminate reference to reductions in out-of-home placements and now simply emphasize the goal of keeping

TABLE 4.7
Locus of Control

SERVICES	DEGREE OF FAMILY CONTROL[a]			
	NONE	A LITTLE	SOME	A LOT
Within the pilot program[b]	6	8	42	63
Outside the pilot program[c]	14	32	56	16

[a] Survey question: "Overall, how much control do you feel you have over the services your family and your child now receive within this program? Outside this program?" [b] 1 missing response. [c] 2 missing responses.

"families together by defraying some of the special costs of caring for a family member at home." Regardless of the benchmark applied, *it can be argued that the program has succeeded in achieving its desired ends.*

While findings related to placement plans may have been confounded by initial program eligibility requirements, results of the survey show over half of those considering an out-of-home placement were *greatly* influenced by the subsidy program to keep their child at home. Very few were not influenced at all. In this sense the subsidy program seems to have succeeded in keeping families together and in reducing the demand for costly out-of-home placements. Only two children in the subsidy program were placed out of home in the first two years of the program.

However, defining the program's efficacy through such a narrow outcome—out-of-home placement—is troublesome. There are those who insist that the subsidy program *must* eventually prove itself in terms of reduced placements out of home and in cost savings to the state. But should services be justified solely on their ability to save tax dollars for the cost of out-of-home placement, or is the goal of improved quality of life for the family as a whole and the person with disabilities in particular a sufficient public good? Preliminary research does suggest that enhanced quality of life of the family—though not directly related to cost savings—does result in substantial benefits to the larger society, including increased family self reliance, maximization of family cohesiveness, and improvements in the productivity of individual family members including the person with disabilities (Dunst, Trivette, & Deal, 1988; Herman, 1983; Perrott & Herman, 1987; Rosenau, 1983). Though these gains are more difficult to measure, they should likewise be part of any systematic exploration of family support practices.

The recent changes enacted by the Iowa legislature affirm the importance of family support to improved quality of life, and the results of the evaluation indicate that, in regard to this goal, the program has also succeeded. Survey results suggest that the program had a positive overall impact on family life. Certainly, the program did not succeed at relieving all family needs and concerns, but families indicated that it improved their lives considerably.

These findings are consistent with those generated through the evaluation conducted by DHS after the program's first year of operation (Cunningham, 1989). The combined data from the two evaluations over two years clearly show a continuing high level of satisfaction with the program and effects consistent with the legislature's intent and beyond.

Question 2: What further issues were raised during the course of the evaluation of the subsidy program?

Two key issues were raised by survey respondents:

Eligibility Requirements. During the program's first year, families complained about (a) the need to have a special education "weight" of 2.2 or 3.6 to qualify for the program, and (b) the requirement that families had to be considering out-of-home placement for their child to be eligible. In response, both criteria have been eliminated.

Still at issue, however, is the amount of family income. To qualify for the program, the family's *taxable* income for the year must not exceed $40,000. Survey findings reveal that in many families at least one member of the household needs to forego employment to provide care at home. The subsidy may make it possible for this person to begin or return to work. But the resulting added income may well push the family over the permitted level, disqualifying the family from the program. For numerous families this represents a "catch 22" and needs to be changed. In Michigan, the state whose cash subsidy served as a prototype for Iowa's effort, the income limit is $60,000.

There was also considerable comment by survey respondents on the program's age limitation of 18 years, as several families were distraught over losing the cash subsidy. This issue is a serious concern of low income families and others who are worried about their capacity to provide care as their child ages.

The subsidy program was designed to provide families with an amount equivalent to the monthly SSI payment of an adult living in the home of another. Once a child turns 18, he or she would receive that amount regardless of his or her family's income, so in a sense the family support subsidy would continue. However, given the fact that nearly *one fourth of the families receiving the subsidy earned less than $10,000 per year and almost one half earned under $20,000,* many of their children were already eligible for SSI. Consequently, ending the subsidy at age 18 can represent a significant financial loss to these families, and the state can expect these families to express continued dissatisfaction with this feature of the program.

Families also worry about their capacity to provide care as their child ages past 18 years. One common expectation held by all parents is that as their child grows into an adult, he or she will also become financially independent. In reality there is often no appropriate place for a family member with a disability to move after the 18th birthday, so large numbers of families must continue to provide care at home. A recent study (Davis, 1987) indicates that at least 2,000 adults with disabilities are already on waiting lists for residential services in Iowa.

The SSI payment their child receives will contribute to his or her financial independence by covering basic living expenses. By law the family support subsidy is not intended to cover basic living costs, but rather the special costs families encounter because of disability. The extra costs of disability do not diminish after age 18—in fact, they may well increase because many programs available to children (e.g., special education, Child Health Specialty Clinics, etc.) are not open to adults. The capacity of parents to provide care also diminishes due to their advancing age and reduced earning capacity as retirement approaches. Even if residential placements are expanded, some families may decide that the quality is unacceptable compared to living at home. Regardless of the cause, there is little doubt that numerous persons with disabilities will continue to live in their families' homes past age 18, and from these families DHS can expect further expression of a need for support.

The Role of the Program within the Larger Human Services System. The subsidy program is administered within a larger human services context where several other services are available to children with disabilities and their families. To date, little effort has focused on how the subsidy fits together with these other pieces to form a comprehensive circle of supports around families. For example, even though regulations prohibit families from using subsidy funds for items that are covered by Medicaid, program families are not provided with specialized information and access to persons within the Medicaid program to ensure that maximum use is made of Medicaid. To make most efficient use of state resources, families must be made aware of all programs and services that might provide them with support.

Conclusion

In summary, the Iowa Family Support Subsidy Program is serving a diverse group of families with multiple needs and concerns. These families expressed general and in some cases overwhelming satisfaction with the administration and impact of the program. Many families had never been eligible for cash assistance before and described the program as a "life saver." While the numerical data offer convincing evidence, the personal comments submitted by many families present a compelling argument for the program. This is perhaps all the more impressive given the newness of the conceptual approach and the emergent character of the program.

However, the data also suggest that there are still needs that are largely unmet by the program, including the lack of a family support consultant to assist in navigating the service system and identifying other resources. For many, the money helped, but only scratched the surface of their needs. Others lamented the fact that their children would soon be over 18 and they would become ineligible, but no less needy.

FAMILY SUPPORT PILOT PROGRAMS IN ILLINOIS

In Illinois, the state's Planning Council on Developmental Disabilities (IPCDD) has demonstrated a deep commitment to families and to the establishment of responsive support systems. One of the objectives stated in the Council's state plan is to develop a statewide system of family supports that utilizes services available within existing state agencies and that enables families to enrich the lives of persons with developmental disabilities while obtaining necessary assistance.

Toward this end, in 1988 the IPCDD allocated $320,000 to fund four pilot family support programs ($80,000 each). Each pilot was to:

- *Develop an advisory board* to provide input and guidance to pilot efforts and to develop a plan of goals and objectives to be accomplished during the course of the project;
- *Provide supports to families by way of information and education,* helping to enable and empower families to receive needed supports, and future planning designed to promote the development of long range plans for their family member; and
- *Establish a financial assistance program* capable of providing families with direct cash payments to purchase needed supports.

In responding to the IPCDD's stated intentions, the four pilot programs proceeded somewhat differently, although they shared common goals and philosophies. In addition, pilot activities at all four sites did not remain static, but evolved as their experience grew. As a result, while the pilots have much in common, there are differences in any number of operational practices (e.g., family selection, needs assessment, distributing financial assistance).

To generate a systematic interpretation of the services provided to the families, the Council sponsored a longitudinal evaluation of the four pilots, which was conducted by the Human Services Research Institute (see Agosta, Knoll, et al., 1991). Evaluation activities began in the winter of 1989 and ended about two years later. *The overall intent of the evaluation was to examine the operation of the pilots in an effort to identify the program practices that are most responsive to the needs of the family.* Three questions were asked:

- Did the four pilot projects achieve program objectives consistent with IPCDD intents?
- How effective were the pilots at addressing family needs?
- What program practices were most responsive to family needs?

Evaluation Methods

Survey Design

The information needed to address these three questions was primarily collected through two mail surveys, spaced about eight months apart, that were directed at participating families. The first mail survey was sent to all families participating in the pilot programs during the spring of 1989 to acquire initial or baseline information on the family member with a disability, family needs, the family's existing sources of support, the family's plans regarding placement of their family member, and other family characteristics.

Much like the form used to complete the Iowa evaluation, the survey took approximately 30 minutes to complete. Both English and Spanish versions were prepared.[3] The four key areas of inquiry were family information, information on the family member with a disability, family needs, and future placement plans.

Beginning in October 1989, the second mail survey was initiated. The form used was nearly identical to the Time 1 form, with these exceptions: Questions considered to be redundant were removed (e.g., items asking about the family member's age or sex or about family income). Questions were added to examine the family's satisfaction with the program, its impact on family life, and placement preferences. Questions were added to inquire about the family's experience with the cash assistance component of the pilots.

Survey Distribution

In this study, *all families who were enrolled with the four pilots prior to April 1, 1989 (166 families) were included.* The survey forms were distributed through staff at each of the four pilots. These staff were each sent a letter

---

[3] A copy of the Illinois Family Support Survey Forms (in English or Spanish) can be obtained through the Human Services Research Institute at 2336 Massachusetts Avenue, Cambridge, MA 02140.

thanking them for their help and providing directions for distributing the survey forms. Also included was a set number of prepared survey packets that site coordinators were instructed to mail to families. Each packet included a letter describing the project, one survey form, and a pre-stamped and addressed envelope for the respondent to return the completed questionnaire.

In a few instances, owing to the circumstances of particular families, pilot staff personally visited families and assisted with the survey's completion. This tactic was deemed appropriate since families were not yet being asked to share their opinion about the pilot's performance in particular.

To track the response pattern, each packet and survey form was given a number (1–166). Pilot staff cross-referenced the numbered forms with particular families. While these codes could be used by pilot staff to identify individual families, the evaluation team did not have access to the cross referenced list. As forms were received, evaluation staff transmitted the code numbers to the site coordinators who, by checking back against the cross-referenced list, could identify particular families who failed to respond to the survey. These families received "reminder postcards" about two weeks after the survey was initiated.

To distribute Time 2 forms, the process noted above was used again. Pilot staff helped to mail either an English or Spanish language form to all families who completed a Time 1 survey. This time, however, owing to the several items requesting information on the impact of the program, pilot staff were not permitted to visit with families to assist with completing the survey form.

Compilation and Analysis

Each returned form was precoded to track return patterns and to simplify the data compilation process. Returned questionnaires first were screened to assess whether the information could be used. Some amount of information was collected on all 166 families in Time 1, given that pilot staff provided some of the data. The number of families actually returning Time 1 survey forms totaled 155 of 166, a response rate of 93%. The Time 2 survey, undertaken some eight months following the first, found 97 of 155 families returning the survey, a response rate of 63%. Figure 4.4 displays the 166 families by pilot site.

Following initial review, data were entered into a microcomputer data base and prepared for analysis through extensive error checks. A specialized data entry program was used to ensure maximum accuracy and efficiency by trained data entry personnel. Once the data were entered, *SPSS PC+* statistics software was used for subsequent analyses.

FAMILIES BY PILOT SITE -- TIMES 1 & 2

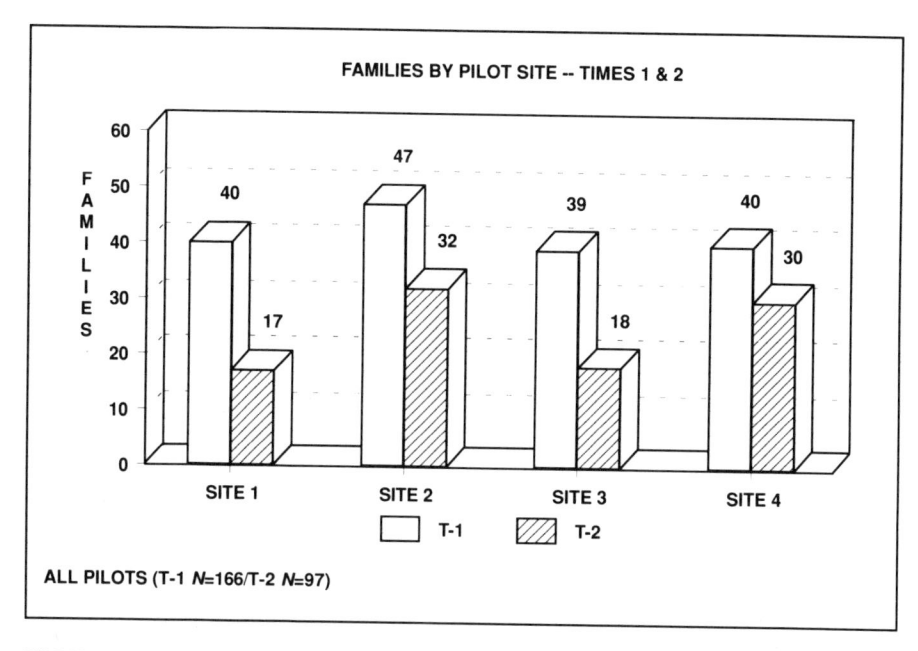

(Bar chart showing counts by site: SITE 1: T-1=40, T-2=17; SITE 2: T-1=47, T-2=32; SITE 3: T-1=39, T-2=18; SITE 4: T-1=40, T-2=30)

ALL PILOTS (T-1 N=166/T-2 N=97)

FIGURE 4.4: Distribution of the families covered in the Time 1 and Time 2 surveys by pilot site.

Evaluation Results: The Two Mail Surveys

After the sampling of respondents' comments, below, frequency counts for many of the items and displays of the some of the scale scores that were computed are discussed in the summary analysis of findings (p. 126). The information is presented in aggregate, and site specific references are not made. The information displayed was gathered from families in response to the Time 1 and Time 2 mail surveys. The maximum number of Time 1 responses totals 166, while the sample for Time 2 included 97 respondents. The great number of "missing cases" noted for Time 2 data reflects the attrition in respondents between the two surveys (69 respondents). In most cases (84% for both Time 1 and Time 2 surveys), the primary respondent was the family member's mother, with other respondents distributed among other family members.

Selected Responses to Open-Ended Questions

A final section of the Time 2 survey form invited respondents to write in their responses to four open-ended questions: (a) What do you most appreciate or value about this family support program? (b) What do you least appreciate about this family support program? (c) What would you do to change how the cash assistance component is run? (d) What would you do to change how this family support program is run? A sampling of the responses follows.

What was appreciated or valued most?

"The time the worker gave to the families in the group. The staff has given me information that I desperately needed. They followed up and showed concern for my family and myself. Their concern was greatly appreciated."

"The assistance from staff members is overwhelming. The support has enabled me to strive as a parent to be an individual advocate for my child's and family's needs."

"The support that has been given to me financially and socially. Just being there to know someone cares about you and understands. I'm thankful for this program."

"It gave us an opportunity to build a ramp which increased our child's safety and lessened physical stress on us."

"That I as a care-giver for 40 odd years, was able to go out and enjoy myself and was able to pay for reliable sitters. Also, our caseworker was most attentive and supportive, and made me feel we were not 'forgotten.'"

"Having enough money for the basics, eased financial worries, reduced stress in our family life, helped us to do things we were not able to do before, helped our family to be more like other families, and improved my ability to care for my 'family member.'"

"They gave me the money for recreation for our disabled child and her sister, which gave me the chance to get them out of the house and we had fun together. Also, the gas company turned off my gas as soon as it got warm out and wanted the whole balance to turn it back on. This program paid for that. The respite program is also good."

"What I most appreciated was how the people went out of their way to be helpful. By helping with much needed services such as public aid and getting food stamps. It's been a big help."

"Our family member was able to get high quality hearing aids that we would not have been able to afford. We can never thank the program enough for this help. The workshops gave us wonderful information about many things we needed to know and helped us to make decisions about our family member. Our caseworker has been extremely helpful and supportive in times of great stress and worry—also great respite help workers."

"The time spent listening to us!"

"The financial help with one of our last larger hospital bills. We also value having the baby-sitter. It gives my husband and I some time to get away once in awhile."

"The person in this program I dealt with was very nice and tried to help us all she could. The help she could provide was limited but appreciated. She was concerned and did all she could."

"The financial assistance given to us to pay off old medical bills. The chance for our child to see a dentist for the first time. The ability to update and change equipment to better meet our child's needs. The caseworker was great and kept close contact with us."

"The personal caring and effort to help us on the part of the program staff."

"Our caseworker has been very appreciated. She goes beyond the call of duty."

"Number one, that the criteria was yearly income of $50,000 and under. A lot of programs, you must be in the extreme poverty level before you can get any kind of assistance. We were able to meet our bills, for the most part, and so could request the moneys for extra things that make our family life more enjoyable."

"The program helped us to the buy equipment we needed to help our child develop due to lack of eyesight and hearing, which helped to reduce a lot of stress. It made it a lot easier for him to learn, and made us see his potential."

"Our family member has had an opportunity to go places and enjoy life more."

"My word was accepted and the kindness and sincerity in actions and the attitude was so nice to see. I have been treated as an equal so there is no way that it is not appreciated. I value it very highly."

What was least appreciated or valued?

"I would like more information or guidelines on how much is available to my son so that I could have been more involved in the budgeting process."

"There was too little time to allow for certain paperwork to get back."

"Paperwork! The process was time consuming and at times stressful."

"We were not able to take full advantage because we could not put out the money to purchase certain items and then wait for reimbursement."

"That more time can be given to research additional information."

"The time it took for the services to be made available to us and the waiting list for the respite program."

"A little more information on available help and how to get it. Help concerning retraining since the family member's surgery and memory loss."

"No results—I feel like I've been left to fight the system alone!"

"We were told we would be allotted a [certain] amount of dollars. When it came down to it, we received less than that. We were led to believe otherwise. I suppose someone else received the rest of the money. Not everyone knows their needs right at first. Ours came up as we went along and when we needed the money it wasn't there."

"The fact that they had based our values [sic] on our income. It doesn't seem fair when both parents try to work and only received so much, and other parents who don't work or won't work and received much more. I feel it should be equally distributed among families."

"The limited amount of funds for this type of program. I feel if there was more money for this program then it may cost less when a child goes to school. A child learns more the first few years of their life, and a parent can teach them more sometimes because they are more at ease. If they had more to work with (learning equipment) at this age, the better off everyone would be."

What should be changed in the cash assistance component?

"If the amount for day-care could be increased it would be helpful."

"I feel the one-time grant was very helpful to meet a specific need, but for long-term benefit to really be felt, an ongoing stipend would be more useful."

"I would send the cash assistance to the family and let them use it as they see fit, and then show the bill to the family support program to show how they used the money."

"I wouldn't change anything. It was fair to try to find other resources in the community for funding before resorting to the pilot project funds."

"A requirement for two to three written proposals before cash is issued is too much for me to handle. Traveling to three different locations to get a written proposal was impossible for me. Therefore the only cash we were granted was for dental work."

"We would do nothing to change the program. We did not actually receive the cash. The payment was made by the agency to the provider. This was very satisfactory and we were very happy about it—and most grateful."

"I would try to give each family what they needed and not what they were only allowed. The income the families made should not be based on the 'family member's' needs. Especially if they have other children in their family."

"When the program first originated, there were only so many families who were discovered as yet who needed the service. The number of families then would receive quite a bit out of the allotted money. Then the number of families eligible grew—but the total money amount stayed the same—so less money per family. Maybe the money allotted could be increased?"

"Spending guidelines should be adjusted to individual needs with the supervisor having the authority to make changes in accordance with the feelings of the board."

"I think the pilot project is doing great. I think people should get a certain amount to each family so everybody will be even and one person doesn't get more than others."

How should the program be changed?

"I wouldn't change a thing—this program has made a positive impact on the life of my retarded son and the rest of my family."

"I would hire more staff members."

"I feel that parents should receive a stipend and should purchase what they feel will help without having to discuss it and map out strategy with someone else unless they want to."

"It would be nice to allot the money and then have the families provide receipts on how it was spent. We are badly in need of a mattress and can't afford to pay for it and then wait to be reimbursed for it."

"Speed up the process for services, make more financial support available to families. Have more workers available to present services to families."

"The follow-through of the surveys. We wanted help with SSI and what other services are available. But we never hear back. The agency is always changing people. It's hard to be followed."

"I would allow each family so much money to run the family [sic]. Cause this year some families got a lot more help than others because they [the program] ran out of money."

"Each family should be allotted the same amount of money. The money should be specifically for that family's needs only, and no one else should be able to take that from that family."

"Let every family know what exactly are the guidelines for the program and be sure they are well understood."

"Establish permanent funding for those in need."

"I would not change it at all. I think it's being run very well."

Summary Discussion of Survey Findings

The Family Member with A Disability

According to survey respondents, the family members served by the four pilots covered a wide range in age, with over half (57%) age 12 or younger. Nearly one-third (29%) were older than age 22. Fifty-nine percent of the family members were male, 41% female. Mental retardation or cerebral palsy was identified as the primary disabling condition by family support staff for over half (55%) of family members, with many other disabilities being represented among the remaining 45%.

When evaluating the impact of their family members' disabilities (Table 4.8), the most often selected choice was "a lot" in mental/intellectual development (48%), physical mobility (35%), communication (42%), and assistance with daily activities (46%). Specialized medical attention was required by many fewer family members; only 16% needed it weekly or daily, while 55% reported they needed it less than monthly. Nearly half (46%) of the respondents reported being challenged by behavior problems less than monthly, while 45% called behavior a weekly or daily challenge. On the whole, the pilots served families with members who have severe disabilities and major support needs.

Families were asked to rate the degree of stress their family member's disability caused, and for the most part the amount of stress was closely related to their perception of the impact of the disability. A notable exception was specialized medical attention, where parental concern was high even among families whose family members seldom required this kind of support. Even when medical emergencies occur rarely, they are potentially so serious that they are a significant cause for chronic worry among many families.

Family Composition and Caregiving

Nearly three-fourths (74%) of family respondents lived in households of four persons or less. For 73%, the family member's mother was the

TABLE 4.8
Impact of the Disability on the Child with the Disability (Time 1)

AREA OF PERFORMANCE AFFECTED	FAMILY PERCEPTIONS OF DEGREE OF IMPACT LEVEL OF DISABILITY[a]	CONCERN FOR DISABILITY[b]	
Mental/intellectual development			
None	15	20	
A little	19	17	
Some	41	41	
A lot	69	64	
Missing	22	24	
Physical mobility			
None	37	30	
A little	24	22	
Some	34	45	
A lot	51	48	
Missing	20	21	
Communication with others			
None	23	24	
A little	15	25	
Some	45	38	
A lot	61	54	
Missing	22	25	
Assistance for daily activities			
None	28	30	
A little	20	21	
Some	32	41	
A lot	68	54	
Missing	18	20	
Specialized medical attention			
Less than monthly	81	20	(None)
Monthly	43	39	(A little)
Weekly	16	42	(Some)
Daily	8	45	(A lot)
Missing	18	20	(Missing)
Challenging behavior			
Less than monthly	64	36	(None)
Monthly	12	30	(A little)
Weekly	27	31	(Some)
Daily	36	45	(A lot)
Missing	27	24	(Missing)

[a] Survey question: "How much/how often does the disability affect performance?" [b] Survey question: "How much concern or stress does it cause?"

primary caregiver. Thirty-six percent were single parent families. As in Iowa, a substantial number of families—one-fourth in this case—included others in the home with significant mental, health, or emotional problems. Forty-two percent of families participating in the pilots earned less than $10,000 per year, and 70% had annual incomes less than $20,000.

TABLE 4.9
Family Opportunity Costs (Time 1)

TO MEET THE NEEDS OF YOUR FAMILY MEMBER WITH A DISABILITY, HAS ANYONE IN YOUR HOUSEHOLD . . .	YES	NO	MISSING
Given up a paying job?	31	103	32
Not looked for a job?	42	85	39
Lost a job because of care demands?	13	114	39
Refused a job transfer or promotion?	10	113	43
Changed jobs for better medical benefits?	7	115	44
Changed jobs for different hours?	13	113	40
Quit school or not gone back?	16	110	40
Lost health insurance coverage?	7	116	43
NOT changed jobs because the change would have meant losing health insurance?[a]	15	69	82

[a] Because this question was asked only during the Time 2 survey, the number of missing cases is high.

Families reported that their family member's disability had contributed to limiting their family income (Table 4.9). One-third of respondents indicated they had not looked for a job due to the demands of caring for their family member at home, and 23% said they had given up a paying job for that reason. Although there is no data for a comparable group of Illinois families without family members with disabilities, these statistics represent a very significant loss of income to families and lost tax revenues to the state. Even families who continue to work experience limitations because of their family member's disability. For example, 18% of respondents said they had not changed jobs because the change would have meant loss of health insurance.

Family Needs

The findings here follow the pattern revealed in the Iowa program (Table 4.10). The areas identified as highest need at Time 1 were planning for future service needs of their family member (55% called it a "very high" need), planning for the future financial security of their family member (51%), planning for what will happen when they can no longer provide care (46%), finding ways to help their family member become more independent (44%), finding opportunities for recreation (41%), and both out-of-home and in-home respite care (42% and 36% respectively).

The Use of Cash Assistance

The data show that cash assistance was not used by all participating families. When it was used, as shown by Table 4.11, it was spent principally on behalf of the family member with a disability for medical services or insurance, transportation, recreation, adaptive equipment and housing adaptations. The only family-centered support purchased with cash assistance was respite.

Locus of Control

There is a significant difference between the amount of control families feel they have over services inside and outside the pilot programs (Table 4.12). Twenty-six percent of respondents said they felt they had no control over services received outside the pilot in the Time 1 survey, while only one respondent (less than 1%) reported an expectation of no control over services within the pilot at Time 1. Forty-four percent of respondents expected to have "a lot" of control over services within the pilot when they entered the program. Experience was even better than expectations: fully 54% reported they had experienced "a lot" of control over the program when they were asked in the Time 2 survey.

Of those families receiving cash assistance, 98% said they had "enough" or "more than enough" control over spending the money. Ironically, 82% of respondents receiving cash assistance reported they thought they were required to spend the cash on their family member with a disability, even though the policy of the family support pilots did not include that limitation. These policies are so different from what families are accustomed to encountering within the human services system that it takes some time for them to be fully understood by families. Once family support policies are clearly communicated and fully grasped, the feelings of control among families should continue to grow.

Influence on Placement Plans

Nearly three-fourths (71%) of respondents indicated they had no plans to seek an out-of-home placement within the next three years at the time they entered the pilot program. This number is a good indicator of family commitment to keeping their family member at home, particularly considering that 29% of family members in the survey were older than age 22. Only 11 (7%) indicated they had requested or were planning to request an out-of-home placement, while 14% reported their family was discussing the issue but had not decided what to do. For those few families seeking an out-of-home placement, a variety of reasons were given. The most common was related to the advancing age of the caregiver and family member with a disability.

When asked how much the family support program had influenced their decision to have their family member continue to live at home, 38% said it had been a moderate to a great influence.

TABLE 4.10
Family Needs Profile (Time 1)

TO WHAT EXTENT DOES YOUR FAMILY HAVE A NEED NOW FOR HELP OR ASSISTANCE:	NOT A NEED			VERY HIGH NEED	MISSING
Having enough money for the basics our family needs or to pay bills	24	19	30	23	53	17
Having a phone	78	18	18	5	26	21
Getting clothing for all family members	55	15	25	27	26	18
Getting information that can tell us about our family member's condition (diagnosis and assessment)	41	28	27	19	34	17
Getting information about the services available	18	14	30	33	54	17
Getting information on how to provide care	37	21	30	22	37	19
Getting information on how I can help make decisions regarding the services our family member receives	39	17	24	28	40	18
Getting financial assistance from government agencies	32	24	25	21	46	18
Finding ways to help our family member become more independent in caring for his or her own needs	46	22	19	16	43	20
Fixing our home to make it easier for our family member to get around	33	13	16	22	65	17
Fixing our home to make it safer for our family member	87	6	17	16	24	16
Transporting our family member around town	84	12	13	16	26	15
Getting special travel equipment (lifts, car seats)	65	10	18	16	42	15
Getting special equipment (wheelchair, language board)	92	9	9	12	26	18
Providing special diet or clothing for our family member	75	12	11	17	33	18
Getting our family member into school or a day program	73	15	23	16	23	16
Finding enough opportunities for our family member to recreate or have fun away from home	78	10	13	8	35	22
Finding enough opportunities for our family member to make friends with persons who do not have a disability	33	16	13	25	60	19
Getting special therapies for our family member (speech, physical, occupational)	57	14	28	14	34	19
Getting counseling for our family member	52	10	19	13	55	17
Getting medical and dental care for our family member	69	12	14	20	30	21
	55	19	16	16	44	16

Finding trained medical professionals who will come to our home to provide care (nurses, home health care)	92	11	6	11	19
Getting adequate health insurance for family member	75	14	15	12	17
Getting someone to come into our house and provide care while I am away	44	13	23	16	17
Getting care for our family member during work hours	88	7	15	3	20
Finding a place away from home where our family member can go when I need a break	42	10	27	8	17
Finding someone to care for our family member in time of a family emergency	44	9	24	14	17
Planning for future service needs of our family member	22	8	16	20	19
Planning for what will happen when we can no longer provide care	48	10	14	9	16
Planning for the future financial security of our family member	20	9	17	27	16
Finding ways to cope with care related stress	28	18	34	15	18
Explaining our family member's disability to others	65	22	23	15	19
Learning how to approach family problems	48	26	34	21	18
Managing a family budget	59	20	28	15	15
Having someone to talk to (family members, friends)	71	15	21	16	16
Finding enough time for myself	30	20	26	22	16
Finding enough time for other family members	47	24	23	26	16
Finding time to complete household chores and routines	47	24	32	12	16
Finding time to socialize with friends	39	22	35	17	17
Vacationing or having fun as a family	35	17	20	25	16
Participating in support groups for parents or other family members	50	28	28	15	16
Getting counselling for parents or other family members	69	17	22	19	16

TABLE 4.11

Items Purchased with the Cash Assistance

SERVICE/ITEM PURCHASED	FREQUENCY OF PURCHASE
Medical and dental expenses	55
Medical insurance	39
Transportation	28
Adaptive equipment	21
Recreation	18
Respite care (in home)	16
Housing adaptations	13
Diagnosis and assessment	10
Therapy (physical, occupational or speech)	10
Home health care	8
Special foods	8
Respite care (out of home)	7
Futures planning (financial or services)	6
Day care	5
Legal services/advocacy	5
Day services (early intervention, special education, vocational)	4
Counseling (family or individual)	3
Homemaker chore services	3
Information and referral	3
Family education	1
Family support groups	1
Case coordination	0

Note. Data was collected from the pilot staff for the pilots' first year of operation.

Impact on Quality of Life

A majority (72%) of respondents reported the program had between "some" and "a great deal" of effect on their family's life, with 28% indicating it had "a great deal" of impact (Figure 4.5). This latter finding may be a reflection of the pilots' emphasis on assisting families to address future financial concerns. Respondents reported the program had a greater impact in some areas than others (Table 4.13). The greatest benefit was improvement in the family's ability to care for the family member with a disability and easing worries about the future well-being of the family member. It had the least impact on financial worries stemming from the family member's disability (38% said it had been of no help in this area). Thirty-two percent of respondents reported the program had been of no assistance in helping their family be more like other families.

The total family impact scale scores indicate that 36% of families reported some impact on their family life, while an equal number (22%) reported very little and a great deal of impact. The remainder (19%) had a moderate impact.

Overall, the degree of impact of the pilots on families responding to the survey reflected programs in their earliest stages of development. Only

TABLE 4.12
Expectations and Locus of Control (Time 1 and Time 2)

SERVICES (TIME)	DEGREE OF CONTROL				
	NONE	LITTLE	SOME	A LOT	MISSING
Overall, how much control do you feel you have over the services received **outside the pilot** (Time 1)	36 (26%)	43 (30%)	36 (26%)	26 **(18%)**	25
Overall, how much control do you feel you have over the services received **outside the pilot** (Time 2)	14 (15%)	28 (30%)	35 (38%)	16 **(17%)**	73
Overall, how much control do you EXPECT to have over the services offered **by the pilot** (Time 1)	1 (1%)	17 (12%)	60 (43%)	61 **(44%)**	27
Overall, how much control HAVE YOU HAD over the services offered **by the pilot** (Time 2)	3 (3%)	13 (14%)	26 (28%)	50 **(54%)**	74

IMPACT ON FAMILY LIFE

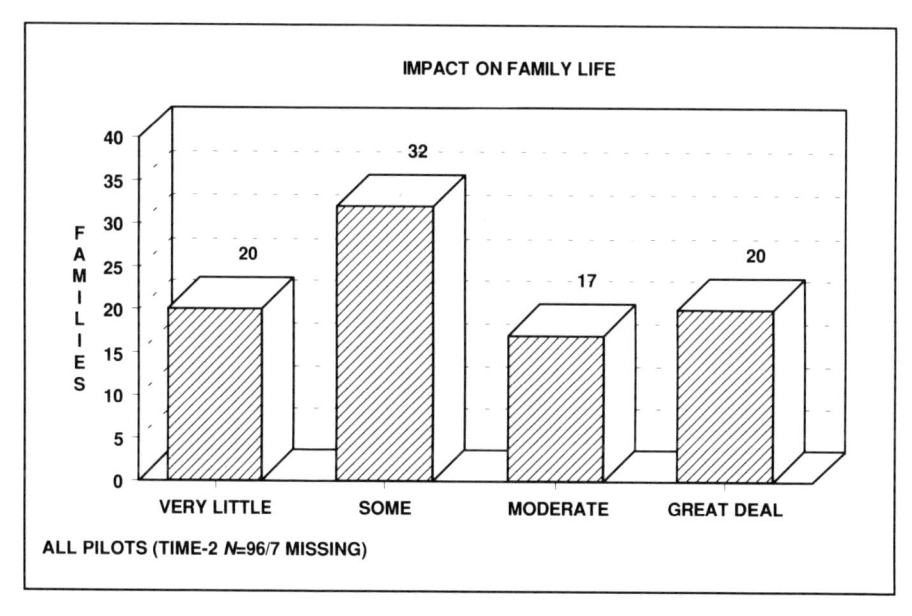

	VERY LITTLE	SOME	MODERATE	GREAT DEAL
FAMILIES	20	32	17	20

ALL PILOTS (TIME-2 N=96/7 MISSING)

FIGURE 4.5: This scale on *total family impact* was developed based on the responses given to the questions displayed in Table 4.13. To create the scale, responses were recoded from 0–4 and then summed to yield a score that could range from 0–36 (4×9). The higher the score, the greater the family impact. The *internal consistency* (measured by the Cronbach alpha statistic) for the 9-item scale was computed at .945.

TABLE 4.13

Impact of the Pilot on Family Life (Time 2)

TYPE OF IMPACT	DEGREE OF IMPACT[a] NOT AT ALL		SOME		A GREAT DEAL	MISSING
Improved your family's life overall	10	16	28	12	26	74
Improved your ability to care for your family member	15	6	32	18	21	74
Helped your family to do more together	21	16	26	13	17	73
Helped your family be more like other families	29	13	20	12	18	74
Eased your financial worries because of your family member	35	16	22	3	17	73
Eased your worries about the future well-being of your family member	14	12	29	15	24	72
Reduced the stress in your family's life	18	21	27	12	15	73
Helped you to do things that you were not able to do before	14	15	34	12	18	73
Helped you to get to know other persons in your community besides other family members	22	9	23	19	20	73

[a] Survey question: "Regarding the program's impact on your family, circle the number that best describes the program's effect."

two-thirds of those responding had received cash assistance from the pilots, and 22% of those receiving cash felt the amount was inadequate. The impact reported at Time 2 should be a more adequate reflection of the pilots' impact on families.

Family Opinion

The overall family satisfaction with the pilot programs as measured by scale scores was overwhelmingly positive (Figure 4.6). Sixty-two percent reported "a great deal" of satisfaction with the programs, with 24% reporting a "moderate" level of satisfaction. Only 4% had "very little" satisfaction. Highest marks were given in the way program staff treated families, with 68% reporting "a great deal" of satisfaction (Table 4.14). Well over half of survey respondents marked the two highest satisfaction selections for each of the categories.

Evaluation Results: Analysis of Longitudinal Effects

The Time 1 and Time 2 surveys, spaced about eight months apart, provided an opportunity to conduct a longitudinal analysis of program effects. Given the range of information collected, multiple indicators of change were examined. What follows is a discussion of the methods used

SATISFACTION WITH THE PILOT

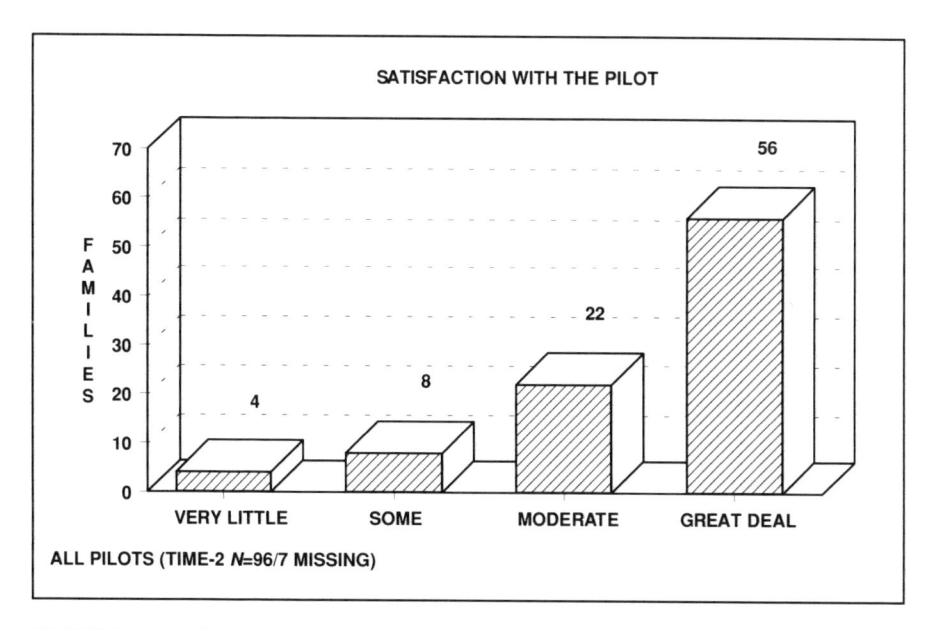

```
70 ┤
60 ┤                                              56
F  50 ┤
A
M  40 ┤
I
L  30 ┤                          22
I
E  20 ┤               8
S
10 ┤     4
 0 └─────────────────────────────────────────────────
     VERY LITTLE   SOME    MODERATE    GREAT DEAL
ALL PILOTS (TIME-2 N=96/7 MISSING)
```

FIGURE 4.6: This scale on *family satisfaction* is based on the responses given to the questions displayed in Table 4.14. To create the scale, responses were recoded from 0–4 and summed to yield a score that could range from 0–24 (4×6). The higher the score, the greater the satisfaction. The *internal consistency* (measured by the Cronbach alpha statistic) for the 6-item scale was computed at .908.

TABLE 4.14

Satisfaction with the Pilot by Item (Time 2)

ASPECT OF PROGRAM	NOT AT ALL		SOME		A GREAT DEAL	MISSING
The application process used for you to get into the program	3	4	14	28	44	73
The information you have received about the program	1	5	14	33	40	73
The process used by staff to develop a services plan for your family	6	5	16	23	42	74
The services offered by the program	5	4	13	26	45	73
The way program staff treated your family	1	2	3	23	64	72
What the program has helped your family to achieve so far	4	5	18	22	42	75

for the analysis, findings stemming from the analysis, and a summary discussion regarding these results.

Method of Analysis

Assessing change with a satisfactory level of statistical credibility is often a difficult task, made more difficult in this particular project by these three factors:

- *The potential insensitivity of child or family related measures to program effects.* Due to the nature of disabilities, service benefits are not always easily or promptly observed. Halpern (1984) suggests that measures may underestimate program effects. Moreover, Weiss (1983) notes that intervention efforts centering on the entire family require that measures be capable of monitoring changes within family dynamics. Such measures have yet to be perfected.

The survey measures used here were newly designed, and while they may have a great amount of face validity, they were not exhaustively field-tested before their use. As a result, the measures' utility for studying change was an unknown.

- *Methodological difficulties associated with longitudinal evaluation.* The lack of immediately observable program effects may suggest that evaluation models be designed to view change over time. Longitudinal evaluation, however, is burdened by a variety of difficulties, including the attrition of participating families, changing service packages received by families, and determining the proper statistical means for assessing change over time (Cronbach & Furby, 1970).

In this study, we observed a significant attrition of families. The number of respondents fell from 166 in Time 1 to 97 in Time 2. In addition, aside from the fact that the pilots each offered a somewhat different package of supports to families, pilot practices were not static, but evolved over time.

- *The relatively short period of time under study.* This project was begun as a 12-month evaluation effort. At best, data on the participating families covered only a 9–10 month period. Given these considerations, observing dramatic change within families due to the supports they received may not be easily accomplished.

Initially, we hoped that by using both Time 1 and Time 2 data, "change scores" for each family and targeted outcome indicator would be calculated. Such scores, referred to as *residual gain scores* (Cronbach & Furby, 1970), are calculated by subtracting the predicted Time 2 score on some targeted dimension (e.g., family stress score) from the actual Time 2 score. The difference acts as a measure of improvement or deterioration that is tied to the initial, Time 1, score. To proceed with this approach, a prediction equation, most likely using multiple regression techniques, must first be constructed based on Time 1 data.

Using this tactic, we proposed to test whether participating families as a group displayed significant changes since Time 1 (baseline). Hypothesizing that if the pilot program had no effect on a family then the family's residual gain score would be zero, an appropriate test of this assertion involves use of the group t test. Each family would be assigned an hypothesized change score of zero (indicating no effect) and this score would be compared to the gain scores using a two-tailed t test. If a significant result were found, we reject the hypothesis that there was no effect and infer that the families were significantly affected by the program.

Limitations in the data obtained, however, do not permit use of this method. For each type of change to be tested, the tactic is dependent on the construction of a multiple regression equation that would allow a credible prediction of Time 2 scores. Given the three factors noted above, the limited number of variables at work and the modest correlations among them that were found, it was not possible to build the required equations. As a result, an alternative option was pursued.

Change was tested by comparing Time 1 and Time 2 scores on particular outcome indicators through use of a "two-tailed" t test. The t-test statistic is a numeric index used to judge the difference in responses between two samples. As the difference grows in magnitude (or reliability), the absolute value of the t-test statistic, or t score, increases. The t score is used, along with consideration of the number of cases involved in the analyses, to assess the statistical reliability of the finding. Generally, "statistically significant" t scores are those where the samples are found to be different and the probability of this difference occurring due to chance is estimated at 5% (.05) or lower.

While this approach is often used, it has limited utility (Bolton, 1979). The approach is based on a comparison of the difference in actual Time 1 and Time 2 scores. However, these scores have the undesirable property of being negatively correlated with initial Time 1 status. That is, persons who score low at Time 1 can only stay low or improve, while those who score high can only stay high or deteriorate. As a result, there is a natural tendency for scores, given repeated measure, to regress toward the mean.

In addition, this type of comparison is undermined by the "unreliability/invalidity dilemma" (Bereiter, 1963). Bolton (1979) writes that "the essence of this dilemma is that the higher the correlation between pretest and posttest administrations of an instrument (which reflects the temporal stability of the variable and suggests that the same construct is being measured), the lower is the reliability of the change scores. Conversely, when the temporal stability is low, implying that the same construct is not being measured at the pretest and posttest administrations ("invalidity"), the reliability of the change score is higher" (p. 106).

Given the circumstances surrounding this study, there is no easy way around these two measurement issues. Indeed, even under the best conditions, assessing change is a troublesome task. However, an approach based on the use of multiple t tests is not entirely without merit. Certainly, comparison of Time 1 and Time 2 samples is useful if only to determine if the measured effects were in the desired direction. And the discovery of statistically significant findings, even while they should be viewed with caution, can inform subsequent research efforts and suggest means for improving programs.

Longitudinal Findings

Only scores involving the 97 families who responded to Time 1 and Time 2 surveys were included in the longitudinal analyses. Comparisons between these 97 families and the 69 others who responded only to the Time 1 survey were also completed for each of the outcome indicators investigated. What follows below are findings resulting from analysis of these three targeted indicators of change: changes in family perceptions of the severity of the family member's disability, family need profiles, and changes in family placement preferences.

Changes in Family and Staff Perceptions of Disability

Families were asked in both the Time 1 and Time 2 surveys to rate the effect of the family member's level of disability along 6 dimensions: mental or intellectual capacity, need for help with daily activities, physical mobility, need for medical intervention, and communication, frequency of challenging behavior.

Respondents made their ratings by circling a number from 1–4. The higher the number circled, the greater the level of severity. For ease of comparison, the distributions show only the responses of the 92 families who participated in both the Time 1 and Time 2 surveys. Given these responses, a series of scales was constructed to measure the total severity of disability perceived by family respondents.

To create the scales, responses were recoded from 0–3 and then summed to yield a score that could range from 0–18 (3×6). The higher the score, the greater the perceived level of disability. The scales were produced for both Time 1 and Time 2 surveys and are displayed by Table 4.15.

In similar fashion, in both Time 1 and Time 2 family respondents were asked to rate the concern or stress the disability causes the respondent along the same six disability dimensions. Following the sequence noted above, a scale was also constructed to measure the total amount of disability

TABLE 4.15
Scales on Perceptions of Disability and Stress ($N = 97$)

SCALE	SURVEY	POSSIBLE RANGE	ACTUAL RANGE	M	SD	INTERNAL CONSISTENCY
Family total severity of disability	Time 1	0–18	0–18	9.57	3.79	.572
Family total severity of disability	Time 2	0–18	3–18	9.43	3.79	.580
Family stress related to disability	Time 1	0–18	0–18	10.72	4.37	.737
Family stress related to disability	Time 2	0–18	0–18	10.53	4.57	.802

related stress experienced by the respondents. This scale could also range from 0–18 (3 × 6), with higher scores indicating higher stress levels. Table 4.15 also displays the properties of the resulting two scale scores.

Comparisons between Time 1 and Time 2 Scale Scores. Table 4.16 displays the findings of all t tests conducted to compare Time 1 and Time 2 scale scores related to perceptions of the family member's level of disability and the family stress experienced.

As shown, statistically significant findings are evident, suggesting that the respondents' overall impressions of their family member's disability improved. The changes were not dramatic, but are positive outcomes worth noting.

Regarding the concern the disability causes the family, no change was observed. Although family perceptions about the level of disability were marginally improved, families experienced no appreciable alleviation in their concern. This is not surprising, given that families often express concern over the future, and modest improvements in one's perception of the disability could not be expected to relieve this worry.

Comparisons between Time 1 Subsamples. One potential problem related to the analysis strategy concerns the attrition in respondents from Time 1

TABLE 4.16
t Tests on Perceptions of Disability and Stress

COMPARISON AND SCALES	CASES	M	SD	t VALUE	2-TAIL PROBABILITY
Family total severity of disability					
Time 1 scale scores	68	10.25	3.64	3.50	.001
Time 2 scale scores	68	9.25	3.80		
Family stress related to disability					
Time 1 scale scores	74	10.89	4.43	1.15	.254
Time 2 scale scores	74	10.48	4.63		

TABLE 4.17
t Tests on Time 1 Perception Subsamples

COMPARISON AND SCALES	CASES	M	SD	t VALUE	2-TAIL PROBABILITY
Family total severity of disability					
Time 1 "Stayers" (n = 97)	68	10.25	3.64	2.21	.029
Time 1 "Leavers" (n = 69)	55	8.74	3.85		
Family stress related to disability					
Time 1 "Stayers" (n = 97)	61	9.69	3.56	.83	.410
Time 1 "Leavers" (n = 69)	65	9.15	3.70		

to Time 2. The full Time 1 sample totals 166 respondents and Time 2 totals 97, a difference of 69 respondents. The *t* tests noted above were keyed only to the 97 cases available in Time 1. If the 69 families who dropped out of the study are significantly different from the comparison sample, then the representativeness of the findings could be questioned.

To test for this difference, the Time 1 sample was divided into two groups; group 1 included the 97 "stayers" and group 2 included the 69 "leavers." The difference between the two groups was examined using *t* tests with Table 4.17 displaying the findings.

The *t* score regarding the family's perception of the level of disability was found to be statistically significant (α = .029). Family respondents who participated in the Time 2 survey ("stayers") perceived, on average, a more severe level of disability than those families who did not participate ("leavers"). The finding suggests that the observed positive impact of the program on family perceptions of disability is tied closely to families whose members have more severe levels of disability.

The *t* score pertaining to the family's perception of the stress or concern caused by the disability was not found to be statistically significant (α = .607). No measured difference was found in the stress felt by families between "stayers" or "leavers."

Conclusions. The evidence suggests that families who participated in the family support programs saw their perception of the family member's level of disability improve. Among families, this finding seems more apt to be observed where disability levels are considered more severe than mild. To contrast, no change in the level of stress or concern felt by families about the disability was observed.

Changes in Family Needs

In both Time 1 and Time 2, families rated their current needs across 43 areas. Table 4.18 displays family responses by item. For ease of comparison, the distributions show the responses of only the 97 families who participated in both the Time 1 and Time 2 surveys. The figure also shows the results of t tests for each item to evaluate the difference between the Time 1 and Time 2 distributions.

Scales on total family needs were developed based on the responses to all 44 items. To create the Time 1 and Time 2 family needs scales, responses were first recoded from 0–4. Second, the responses for each respondent across all 44 areas were summed to yield a score that could range from 0–176 (4 × 44). The higher the score, the greater is the overall level of family need. Table 4.19 displays the properties of the resulting two scale scores.

Comparisons between Time 1 and Time 2 Item Distributions. Table 4.18 shows the results of t tests that compare responses for 43 potential needs. The figure shows the number of cases used in the analysis, the t-test score and the two-tail probability associated with the score. Probabilities found to be .05 or lower are considered "statistically significant," and these are highlighted in bold print.

Nearly all the t-test scores are positive numbers, and statistical differences between Time 1 and Time 2 distributions were found for nine items. These items cluster around (a) getting information to families, (b) getting specialized supports for the family member (e.g., equipment, diet, therapies), (c) providing family care givers with a break (i.e., respite), and (d) easing worry over the future.

Comparisons between Time 1 and Time 2 Scale Scores. Table 4.19 displays the findings of the t test conducted to compare Time 1 and Time 2 scale scores related to family needs. As shown, the finding was statistically significant ($\alpha = .001$), suggesting that those who participated in the pilots experienced an overall real decline in their needs.

Comparisons between Time 1 Subsamples. Differences between the Time 1 subsamples of "stayers" and "leavers" were again tested; this time the test was keyed to family needs. To test for this difference, the Time 1 sample was divided into groups; group 1 included the 97 "stayers" and group 2 included the 69 "leavers." The difference between the two groups' family needs scores for Time 1 was examined using a t test. The bottom half of Table 4.20 displays the results of this test. No statistically significant difference was found between the two samples.

Conclusions. The findings suggest that participation in the pilots was related to a significant decline in family needs. This was certainly a desired program outcome. The finding, however, should not be taken to imply that all family needs were alleviated. Indeed, even after their participation families expressed a great array of needs. Yet, the finding is positive and indicates that the pilot efforts likely had a favorable impact on families.

TABLE 4.18
Family Needs Profile (Time 1 and Time 2) Using Time 2 Sample ($N = 97$)

TYPE OF NEED	TIME 1 SURVEY NOT A NEED	TIME 1 SURVEY NEED	TIME 1 SURVEY VERY HIGH NEED	TIME 1 SURVEY MISSING	TIME 2 SURVEY NOT A NEED	TIME 2 SURVEY NEED	TIME 2 SURVEY VERY HIGH NEED	TIME 2 SURVEY MISSING	COMPARISON CASES	COMPARISON t SCORE	p
Having enough money for the basics our family needs or to pay bills	12	11	20	14	37	3	16	8	16	32	7	87	.77	.444
Having a phone	48	10	15	4	16	4	55	6	6	10	15	5	88	-.32	.749
Getting clothing for all family members	32	10	18	18	17	2	25	11	26	13	16	6	89	-.25	.804
Getting information that can tell us about our family member's condition	24	17	21	16	18	1	37	14	15	10	16	5	91	2.50	.014
Getting information about the services available	14	6	18	22	35	2	19	12	17	19	26	4	91	2.57	.012
Getting information on how to provide care	23	11	18	17	24	4	38	15	10	10	20	4	89	3.47	.001
Getting information on our family member's legal rights	21	11	13	22	29	1	25	9	21	10	28	4	92	1.60	.112
Getting information on how I can help make decisions regarding the services our family member receives	18	17	15	14	30	3	25	14	17	18	19	4	90	1.70	.093
Getting financial assistance from government agencies	26	10	14	11	32	4	30	12	8	11	31	5	88	.63	.533
Finding ways to help our family member become more independent in caring for his or her own needs	24	6	10	12	43	2	25	10	19	10	28	5	90	2.26	.026
Fixing our home to make it easier for our family member to get around	56	5	9	11	15	1	52	6	12	10	12	5	91	.06	.950
Fixing our home to make it safer for our family member	56	6	7	11	16	1	46	13	11	8	15	4	92	-.34	.736
Transporting our family member around town	40	7	9	13	27	1	35	9	19	12	18	4	92	1.04	.299
Getting special travel equipment (lifts, car seats)	60	6	3	9	16	3	64	4	6	10	9	4	90	1.20	.234
Getting special equipment (wheelchair, language board)	47	7	6	11	23	3	51	10	8	7	15	6	88	2.45	.016
Providing special diet or clothing for our family member	42	10	14	11	18	2	52	10	5	9	15	6	89	2.65	.010
Getting our family member into school or a day program	52	8	9	4	18	6	58	6	5	4	18	6	86	.98	.332
Finding enough opportunities for our family member to recreate or have fun away from home	25	7	9	13	39	4	25	9	11	14	32	6	87	1.58	.117
Finding enough opportunities for our family member to make friends with persons who do not have a disability	39	6	17	8	23	4	38	11	9	10	23	6	87	.13	.896
Getting special therapies for our family member (speech, physical, occupational)	35	6	12	9	32	3	38	11	8	8	24	8	88	2.22	.029
Getting counseling for our family member	47	9	4	10	21	6	52	11	7	5	13	9	82	1.53	.131

Getting medical & dental care for our family member	29	13	10	10	34	1	38	6	8	6	33	6	90	.75	.453
Finding trained medical professionals who will come to our home to provide care (nurses, home health care)	63	6	4	6	15	3	60	9	5	5	13	5	90	.63	.390
Getting adequate health insurance for family member	46	9	8	10	22	2	47	9	9	4	21	7	88	.86	.390
Getting someone to come into our house and provide care while I am away	27	6	17	9	35	3	40	4	13	13	22	5	89	2.97	**.004**
Getting care for our family member during work hours	56	3	6	2	25	5	49	10	9	6	17	6	87	.78	.435
Finding a place away from home where our family member can go when I need a break	27	5	14	5	43	3	30	7	10	10	33	7	87	1.91	.059
Finding someone to care for our family member in time of a family emergency	28	6	15	9	37	2	33	7	14	7	31	5	90	1.65	.101
Planning for future service needs of our family member	12	3	12	16	51	3	10	13	19	11	38	6	88	2.38	**.019**
Planning for what will happen when we can no longer provide care	31	5	8	7	45	1	31	10	13	5	33	5	91	2.16	**.033**
Planning for the future financial security of our family member	12	6	10	19	48	2	10	11	20	17	36	3	92	1.69	.094
Finding ways to cope with care related stress	15	13	23	9	35	2	24	17	12	13	28	3	92	1.84	.070
Explaining our family member's disability to others	38	15	16	10	15	3	46	17	12	7	12	3	91	1.81	.074
Learning how to approach family problems	25	19	20	15	14	4	34	14	23	10	13	3	90	1.50	.137
Managing a family budget	37	14	17	9	19	1	41	15	13	15	10	3	93	1.46	.147
Having someone to talk to (family members, friends)	42	12	10	10	21	2	43	16	13	5	16	4	91	1.25	.213
Finding enough time for myself	18	12	18	15	32	2	19	10	18	17	30	3	92	.43	.671
Finding enough time for other family members	27	17	16	17	19	2	29	12	20	17	16	3	92	.76	.449
Finding time to complete household chores and routines	32	15	20	8	20	2	34	14	16	16	15	2	93	.37	.711
Finding time to socialize with friends	20	16	25	8	26	2	30	11	21	14	19	2	93	1.40	.165
Vacationing or having fun as a family	18	11	14	17	35	2	24	8	11	21	30	3	92	1.16	.250
Participating in support groups for parents or other family members	27	19	19	10	20	2	31	17	16	17	13	3	92	1.19	.237
Getting counselling for parents or other family members	44	10	11	14	16	2	43	15	15	12	9	3	92	1.56	.123

TABLE 4.19

Scales on Family Needs Profiles

SCALE	SURVEY	POSSIBLE RANGE	ACTUAL RANGE	M	SD	INTERNAL CONSISTENCY
Total Family Needs Scale	Time 1	0–176	11–160	78.57	36.14	.9422
Total Family Needs Scale	Time 2	0–176	8–153	72.07	36.28	.9427

Changes in Placement Preferences

Family placement preferences were examined for Time 1 and Time 2 using much the same question. No statistical analysis was undertaken regarding this issue because there was relatively little variance to inspect. Regardless of the survey period, families overwhelmingly preferred to keep their family member home. Relatively few were seeking or considering an out-of-home placement. Not surprisingly then, these data also suggest that there was little overall change concerning placement preferences.

Summary Discussion Concerning the Longitudinal Analyses

The longitudinal analyses presented above are by no means meant to be conclusive. Change is a difficult concept to assess, made more difficult in this case by the short time span under study and limitations imposed by the number and nature of the survey questions used.

These cautions aside, the findings presented above are quite favorable. Positive changes were observed concerning both family perceptions regarding the family member's overall level of disability and the overall level of family needs. Little change, if any, was observed with regard to family placement preferences, but this finding must be considered in light of the overall preference of families for continued care at home.

TABLE 4.20

t Tests on Family Needs Scales

COMPARISON AND SCALES	CASES	M	SD	t VALUE	2-TAIL PROBABILITY
Total Family Needs Scales					
Time 1 Scale Scores	86	81.82	36.14	3.36	.001
Time 2 Scale Scores	86	72.08	36.93		
Total Family Needs Scales					
Time 1 "Stayers" (n = 97)	86	81.82	36.14	1.34	.182
Time 1 "Leavers" (n = 69)	55	73.49	35.88		

In judging the performance of the pilots, however, these outcomes should not be considered alone, but should be viewed together with all other findings gained through the survey, including family opinions about the program and its impacts (see Tables 4.13 and 4.14 and Figures 4.5 and 4.6) and the testimony provided through response to the open-ended questions. By using all the available data, overall conclusions based on a convergence of findings can be used to assess the pilots' performance.

Discussion Relevant to the Three Evaluation Questions

Question 1: Did the four pilot projects achieve program objectives consistent with the specifications of the IPCDD?

These family support pilots were to develop an advisory board, provide supports to families by way of information and education, and establish a financial assistance program.

For the most part, the pilots substantially met their stated objectives. Each pilot proceeded in ways consistent with achieving these initial intentions. Advisory boards and cash assistance programs were established, and "case managers" set about the business of supporting families. In fact, as evidenced by Table 4.18, the pilots significantly reduced family needs in areas that the IPCDD had specifically targeted. The areas that seemed most positively addressed cluster around getting information to families, acquiring specialized supports for the family member (e.g., equipment, diet, therapies), providing family caregivers a break (i.e., respite), and easing worry over the future.

However, the issue is more complicated than that. Several program objectives targeted rather elusive concepts, such as "family empowerment" or "program flexibility." While the pilots worked to translate these concepts into practice, the extent to which they succeeded is open to question. Families seemed to have mixed experiences. Many had positive experiences, and felt in control of a flexible array of supports. In fact, Table 4.12 displays powerful evidence that the families who participated in the pilots had great control over the supports they received, a finding made more salient when it is compared to the control families felt they had over supports external to the pilots. In addition, an impressive array of family supports was documented.

Other family respondents, however, seemed less sure of their experiences and wished for something more. Some families felt that they were being "judged" and that they were not encouraged to play an empowered role. Others felt that the supports offered did not truly address their needs. While these findings may in part be due to start-difficulties, they serve notice that "helpgiving" is a complicated task that requires staff to continually inspect and reform program practices as improved means are found or as individual circumstances warrant.

Question 2: How effective were the pilots at meeting family needs?
Over the course of the pilots, program staff met with families and coordinated the delivery of a significant array of supports. But were these activities effective? Were family needs addressed?

Results of this study strongly suggest that *to the extent feasible the pilots were effective at meeting family needs.*

- Information collected during the Time 2 survey clearly documents that families were *highly satisfied* with the pilots (Table 4.14) and that the pilots had a *favorable impact* on various facets of family life (Table 4.13).
- The longitudinal findings suggest that the pilots *helped improve family perceptions* regarding the severity of their family member's disability (Table 4.16), *significantly reduced family needs* (Table 4.18), and likely *helped solidify a strong commitment* among families for continued care at home.
- The handwritten responses to open-ended questions provided by families indicate that, overall, families were enormously appreciative of the help they received, and more than one urged state decision makers to expand the programs so that others could be helped.

As favorable as these findings are, however, this is not to say that the pilots were fully successful in addressing *all* family needs. Survey results (Table 4.18) also indicate that a great array of needs were left unmet. Many such needs, pertaining to health insurance, public school services, or chronic poverty, for example, fell outside the bounds of these family support programs. Full realization of these programs' potential, then, would likely require reform in other facets of the Illinois system of supports, resulting in a more cohesive response to family needs that is not solely dependent upon the actions of any single program (see Agosta, Deatherage, & Bradley, 1991).

Question 3: What program practices were most responsive to family needs?
Overall, survey findings suggest that families were generally satisfied with how the programs went about responding to their needs. Several family members made clear that they appreciated how they were treated by pilot staff and gave special notice to the respect they were accorded and the effort made to act upon family requests. These findings suggest that *just as important as the services offered is how such services are designed and delivered* (Dunst et al., 1988).

Within this context, the evaluation findings suggest that the most responsive program practices are those that—

- *maximize the family's control over the services and materials they receive.* Such control should not be limited to that which is exerted by families on their individual circumstances, but should also include means for involving them with the design and administration of the overall family support network. While families may not seek to be burdened by day-to-day administrative demands, their combined voices should help to shape the program and guide its direction.
- *are offered in ways to minimize the cost to the family for seeking and acquiring help.* By "cost" we are not just thinking of money. Costs can be thought of in other ways as well, such as emotional turmoil or heartache, or the personal time of a family member. If family members believe that the cost they must pay to gain entry to or be involved with a program is too high, they may well choose not to participate.
- *recognize and nurture the caregiving role family members play, providing supports to all members of the family unit.*
- *are flexible enough to accommodate the unique needs of individual families*, offering families multiple options from which to choose and means for honoring unusual requests.

In placing these concepts into practice, two program features that carried the most promise were the constructive role played by "case managers" and the cash assistance programs administered by the pilots.

The Role Played by "Case Managers".[4] Each program sought to provide families with "information and education" keyed to each family's preferences and stated needs. For the most part, delivery of this type of support was based on the interaction between individual families and the "case manager." From the start these persons were charged with enacting a new way of interacting with families, one based on IPCDD's guiding principles and several of the "best practice" concepts noted above.

Playing this new role well did not always come easily or quickly. Numerous case managers were just learning about or testing these concepts even as the pilots began operations. Our impression was that it took some time for case managers to fully embrace their new role.

Not surprisingly, families had mixed experiences. Several were enthusiastic in their evaluation of the person acting as their "case manager," revealing a sense of genuine collaboration based on a deliberate effort to take seriously the needs and preferences expressed by families. Yet a few others reported problems with case management, complaining that case managers were too judgmental or did not provide sufficient information.

---

[4]In several states, the label "case manager" is not used in family support programs because the words emphasize that the professional rather than the family is in the lead. Titles such as "family consultant" or "family agent" are used instead. In fact, in several pilots labels other than "case manager" were used to designate the roles these persons played.

The weight of the evidence suggests, however, that ultimately the case managers played an essential role in the pilots' success. In this regard, the verbal comments offered by families provides ample documentation of their value. Consider again these family comments:

"The assistance from staff members is overwhelming. . ."

"Our caseworker was most attentive and supportive, and made me feel we were not 'forgotten'."

"Our caseworker has been extremely helpful and supportive in times of great stress and worry."

"The person in this program I dealt with was very nice and tried to help us all she could."

"Our caseworker has been very appreciated. She goes beyond the call of duty."

Families truly appreciated the help offered by the case managers. And such help was provided in ways that placed the control in the hands of families (see Table 4.12). Given the current concern for empowering families, this latter finding cannot be overemphasized.

The Cash Assistance Programs. By the end of the 1980s, some 27 states offered families some form of cash assistance (Knoll et al., 1990). The value of this approach is twofold: It offers families a way to acquire goods or services that are not typically available through traditional service structures, and it provides families with the flexibility required to offset various costs of living or to enhance the overall quality of family life (Agosta, 1989). Yet cash assistance programs are often the topic of lively debate over how they should be administered and made accountable.

Within these pilots, the cash assistance program was not made available to all the participating families. Instead, it was portioned out according to rules developed within each pilot. Typically, families received varying amounts, depending on available program funds and according to their needs.

There is no doubt that the cash assistance feature of the pilots was a great help to families, as is evidenced by the vast array of supports that were purchased and the appreciative comments offered by families. However, families did not always agree with how this feature of the pilots was administered. Their comments seem to reflect an ongoing and unresolved disagreement over finding a way to distribute financial assistance that is at once least intrusive to families and also equitable and accountable.

CONCLUSION

Several issues emerge from these two evaluations. First, the two studies strongly suggest that cash subsidy is very helpful to families, but that families also value the assistance of a family consultant or case manager to help them to negotiate the system and to provide them with advice, when needed, on the options available to them. Further, the way in which this help is offered is also very important. Families clearly value help givers who see their roles as partners and facilitators rather than as "managers" of families.

These results also highlight the fact that family support programs in isolation cannot meet all of the needs of families of children with disabilities. Families rely on a range of formal and informal and public and private supports that are rarely knit together and that can thwart the efforts of the family to find resources to meet their needs. The importance of coordination among these various entities—though a truly formidable task—should be a primary part of any policy agenda even once a family support program is put into place.

These two studies also suggest that most families will maintain their children at home, and though the presence of family support may head off some out-of-home placements, the primary benefit of family support is enhancement of the quality of life of the family. This enhanced quality of life can in turn have material benefits to the economy in terms of an expanded wage-earning capacity, the return to the work force of the care giver, and so forth. However, "selling" family support based on the more dramatic cost trade-offs involved in avoiding institutional placement is somewhat misleading.

Further, family support should not presume that all children with disabilities must or can remain at home. An eventual separation between a child and his or her parents is natural. Additionally, for some small number of families, the challenge of care may be too great and no amount of support sufficient to prevent placement out of the home. In such cases, the aim should be to place the child in a foster, adoptive, or specialized family care arrangement.

Finally, a variety of considerations are involved in determining eligibility requirements for family support programs. What should the income cut-offs be? And should the program be limited to children under 21 years of age? Many people with disabilities remain in the family home long after their twenty-first birthday, and as many of these families already receive SSI, there may be some value in continuing to assist families to care for their family members as long as such support does not jeopardize the ultimate independence of the person with a disability.

REFERENCES

Agosta, J. (1989). Using cash assistance to support family efforts. In G. Singer & L. Irvin (Eds.), *Support for caregiving families: Enabling positive adaptation to disability*. Baltimore: Brookes.

Agosta, J., Deatherage, M., Keating, T., Bradley, V., & Knoll, J. (1990). *Families who have children with disabilities and the Iowa Family Subsidy Program: Evaluation findings*. Des Moines: Iowa Planning Council on Developmental Disabilities.

Agosta, J., Knoll, J., Freud, E., Osuch, R., White, C., Rabb, B., & Godfrey, T. (1990). *Four pilot family support programs funded by the Illinois Planning Council on Developmental Disabilities: Evaluation findings*. Chicago: Illinois Planning Council on Developmental Disabilities.

Agosta, J., Deatherage, M., & Bradley, V. (1991). *Toward building a comprehensive system of family supports in Illinois: The state of the state*. Chicago: Illinois Planning Council on Developmental Disabilities.

Bereiter, C. E. (1963). Some persistent dilemmas in the measurement of change. In C. Harris (Ed.), *Problems in measuring change*. Madison: University of Wisconsin Press.

Bolton, B. (1979). *Rehabilitation counseling research*. Baltimore: University Park Press.

Cronbach, L., & Furby, L. (1970). How should we measure "change"—or should we? *Psychological Bulletin*, 74, 68–80.

Cunningham, S. T. (1989). *Evaluation report on family support subsidy program*. Des Moines: Iowa Department of Human Services, Division of Mental Health, Mental Retardation and Developmental Disabilities.

Davis, S. (1987). *A national status report on waiting lists of people with mental retardation for community services*. Arlington, TX: Association for Retarded Citizens of the United States.

Dunst, C., Trivette, C., & Deal, A. (1988). *Enabling and empowering families: Principles and guidelines for practice*. Brookline, MA: Adeline Books.

Halpern, R. (1984). Lack of effects for home based early intervention? Some possible explanations. *American Journal of Orthopsychiatry*, 54(1), 33–42.

Herman, S. E. (1983). *Family support services: Reports on meta-evaluation studies*. Lansing: Michigan Department of Mental Health.

Iowa Legislative Statute, 1988, 225C.36.

Knoll, J., Covert, S., Osuch, R., O'Connor, S., Agosta, J., and Blaney, B. (1990). *Family support services: An end of decade status report*. Cambridge, MA: Human Services Research Institute.

Parrott, M. E., & Herman, S. E. (1987). *Report on the Michigan family support subsidy program*. Lansing: Michigan Department of Mental Health.

Rosenau, N. (1983). *Final evaluation of a family support program*. Macomb-Oakland, MI: Macomb County Community Mental Health and Macomb-Oakland Regional Center.

Singer, G., & Irvin, L. (Eds.) (1989). *Support for caregiving families: Enabling positive adaptation to disability*. Baltimore: Brookes.

Weiss, H. (1983). Issues in the evaluation of family support and education programs. *Family Resource Coalition Report*, 2(4), 10–11.

Chapter 5

Family Empowerment
Four Case Studies

Marsha Langer Ellison
Hank Bersani, Jr.
Bruce Blaney
and
Elissa Freud

INTRODUCTION

This chapter describes the results of case studies of four demonstration programs. In 1988, the Pennsylvania Developmental Disabilities Planning Council tested the effectiveness of family support practices based on family empowerment principles practices by funding four 2-year pilot programs. The ultimate aim was to determine whether these demonstrations could form the basis of principles and practices for a permanent family support agenda in the state.

The four pilot programs were designed for children with a range of disabling conditions such as emotional disturbances or medical or physical disabilities who did not also have mental retardation. Two projects targeted the needs of families with children with mental illness or emotional disorders. These were sponsored by local mental health associations—one urban, one rural. Both had minimal staff and resources and were devoted to advocating for and educating families. They both used parent support groups and educational forums. The projects differed insofar as the specific activities sponsored and the administration of the cash assistance component.

The other two projects were located in Philadelphia. Both targeted families with a child with a physical or medical disability. In one pilot, families were eligible if they had abused or neglected their children or were at risk of neglecting or abusing their children. These two pilots, operated

---

Acknowledgment. The case studies described here were sponsored through a grant provided by the Pennsylvania Developmental Disabilities Planning Council. All opinions expressed herein are solely those of the authors and do not reflect the position or policy of the Pennsylvania Developmental Disabilities Planning Council. The full text of the four case studies is available from the Council in Harrisburg, Pennsylvania.

by private nonprofit agencies, employed a traditional casework approach to the families, utilizing professional social workers.

All four pilots operated on a first come, first served basis with few other eligibility criteria. Each served families from a range of socioeconomic and ethnic backgrounds, although the majority of families served in the two Philadelphia pilots were people of color who were receiving public assistance.

Each pilot responded in a different way to the following service components:

Parent Advisory Council—composed of parents with a child with a disability, these councils were intended to guide and inform the pilot implementation;

Core Services—such things as information and referral, respite services, in-home education, and parent training;

Case Consultant—an individual who linked families with local human services resources and informal networks and who was knowledgeable about interpersonal dynamics and committed to empowering and supporting the family; and

Financial Assistance—a "line of credit" available to families, which was premised on the recognition that the care of children with disabilities exceeds the average costs of childrearing and that families have the financial assistance coming as "their due" with "no strings attached."

EVALUATION METHODOLOGY

The independent evaluation of the pilots was conducted by the Human Services Research Institute (HSRI) and supported by the Pennsylvania Council. The evaluators were charged with answering the following questions:

1. What were the overall characteristics of the four pilots, their activities, and the families they served?
2. Did the projects demonstrate whether linkages to supports assisted families to care for their children at home?
3. What was the experience of families and pilot staff regarding—
    family empowerment principles?
    the cash components?
    linking families to supports?
    family satisfaction with services?
4. What was the impact of the pilots on the attitudes and practices of staff, and did it affect the service environment?
5. What are the implications of the pilots for family support policy?

To answer these questions, the evaluators adopted a qualitative research design.[1] Data were collected through in-depth, in-person and telephone interviews with a large sample of families served in each project. The samples ranged from 10% in one pilot, which had less intensive involvement with a large number of families, to the universe of families served in another pilot, which had more intense involvement with a smaller number of families. The interviews were open-ended though guided by an interview protocol. Interviews were also conducted with all relevant pilot staff and administrators and with a sample of members of the parent advisory councils. Relevant documents were also reviewed. Findings were collected and written into a single case study for each pilot.

FINDINGS

Many of the individual pilot findings and recommendations were relevant but somewhat idiosyncratic. However, taken together, the four case studies are instructive about key features of family support programs in general and provide information about ways to expand family support efforts. The key findings across the four pilots are as follows:

- A key feature of support is *parent-to-parent affiliation*.
- Pilots were highly successful in *linking parents* with specialized and generic resources and in *advocating for and educating parents*, all of which greatly enhanced parents' capacities to care for their child with disabilities at home.
- Effective family empowerment depends on *skilled and knowledgeable staff*.
- The *wider professional community needs education* in the principles of family empowerment.
- *Respite services*, though urgently needed, *are constrained* by logistical and other difficulties.
- *Allowing services to be driven by the family is highly successful* in that services are expressly tailored to individual needs, and these practices are very empowering.
- Only highly *individualized services can best meet the needs of families* whose range of needs is as diverse as the disabling conditions of the children they care for.
- *Financial assistance is a meaningful way to help families cope* with raising a child with a disability.

---

[1] A discussion of the appropriateness of a qualitative case study design for these types of questions can be found in *Case Study Research: Design and Methods* (Applied Social Research Series, Vol. 5), 1984, by R. Yin, 1984, London: Sage.

- Families demonstrated that if allowed to spend the cash on whatever they choose, *they can be trusted to use the cash in appropriate ways.*
- *Parent advisory councils were highly successful* as vehicles for personal growth for the participating individuals and as mechanisms by which programs can better reflect the needs and interests of families.
- *Associations of parents are powerful vehicles for family support;* however, more traditional service providers can also be highly empowering and effective.
- Despite the efforts of the Developmental Disabilities Council, *the time-limited nature of the demonstration caused considerable personal loss* for some participants, suggesting that greater care must be exerted regarding the continuation of future demonstration programs.

Parent-to-Parent Affiliation

Three of the four pilot programs actively developed parent support groups, usually tied to educational efforts and professional presentations. Parent-to-parent affiliation also occurred through the parent advisory councils and other project activities. The tremendous relief and inspiration that parents found in each other's company were a common theme across these three case studies, and for many parents this aspect of their experience was the principal benefit. Their association with other parents let them know that "they were not alone," it helped to reduce the stigma they experienced, and it gave them the support and guidance necessary to challenge systemic barriers to their child's welfare. For some it produced a lasting network of friendship and informal support resources and a sense of community and family in an otherwise reduced social support network. For others it enhanced their self-esteem and their ability to help others. Parents spoke of renewed hope and strengthened ability to continue coping with the daily impact of raising a child with disability.

While this finding is not unexpected, that this was the key feature of support for many parents was surprising. This is not to say that parent support groups were flawlessly implemented. Significant logistical difficulties were experienced by all of the groups, especially with respect to physical locations and scheduling, and in many groups, attendance wavered or tapered off. Findings were mixed about how, and to what extent, professional leadership of the groups would have ameliorated some of the difficulties encountered. In addition, one parent group struggled with issues of class and racial diversity, as well as differences created by variations in the severity of their children's disabilities. In addition, it is important to note that support groups are not for everybody, and they do not substitute for other more instrumental features of family support. Nonetheless, the benefit derived by those parents who did attend the groups was reported to be immeasurable.

Individualized Advocacy, Education, and Service Coordination

A variety of other activities carried out by the pilots also ranked high by families. The pilots were quite successful in linking parents with specialized and generic community resources for themselves and their children. All pilots educated parents about their rights and the possibilities for addressing their needs. Pilot staff advocated for families by addressing bureaucratic entanglements for them, by accompanying them to important meetings, by obtaining the wherewithal families needed to get by, and sometimes by simply providing telephone numbers of places where families could obtain other assistance.

The pilots did this through a number of methods. Some used traditional social casework involving in-home periodic visits by trained social workers, others used pilot staff who committed much of their time to individual problem solving and advocacy, and one used a 24-hour hot line. Whatever the method, the result was that parents felt that they had access to someone who cared, who was available to them without trying to control or manipulate them, and who was truly knowledgeable and capable. Sometimes the achievements were as concrete as obtaining permanent housing for a homeless family or as evanescent as lifting a parent's spirit by listening without judgment. In any case it was clear that the quality of the families' lives was greatly amplified both by the resources garnered and by the availability of a sympathetic ear.

Skilled and Knowledgeable Staff

While individualized advocacy and service coordination are key, the pilot case studies show that this service depends on the quality of the staff performing it. Although staff persons who themselves had a family member with a disability had a head start in understanding the families' dilemmas, this should not be construed as a requirement. What seemed most important, aside from a well developed knowledge base of resources, family rights, and system procedures, was an individual who genuinely embraced family-centered, family empowering practices.

Educating the Wider Professional Community in Family Empowerment

An interesting finding emerging from an assessment of the context of the pilots was the reluctance of professionals outside the pilots to embrace family empowerment principles. In both "mental health" pilots, referral sources (schools, clinics, physicians) deliberately refused to refer families to the pilots. They labelled the programs as therapy groups aimed at alleviating parental guilt. Pilot staff also suspected some unconscious bias on the part of referral sources who referred more white middle class families to an agency that more typically received referrals of low income minority families. This suggested that the message of family empowerment is still new, and it takes time and concerted educational activities to accomplish attitudinal changes.

Respite Services

Three of the pilots sought to make respite services available to families. All respite programs attempted were so beset by implementation difficulties that none can be termed truly successful. The litany of difficulties may sound familiar to observers of respite efforts across the country, including unavailability of respite at the times or places that families require it, respite workers having no personal transportation, inability to respond promptly to sudden family needs, workers who are over or under trained, inability of families to identify their own respite worker, presence of sociocultural gaps between respite workers and the families employing them, liability concerns, bureaucratic barriers to flexible respite, high rates of turnover among respite workers, and fear among workers of making home visits in crime ridden neighborhoods. Unfortunately, the pilots shed no light on how these difficulties can be overcome, while the urgency for respite care is unabated. Plans for expanded, flexible, individualized respite must proceed with an understanding that further experimentation and evaluation are needed to solve these difficulties.

Family-Driven Services

All of the pilots were based on the assumption that the family knows best what services they need, and the four pilots had varying rates of success in fully incorporating this principle into their practices. However, the evidence is clear that, to the extent that the pilot allowed families to choose and define the services they needed, (a) families were well able to articulate their need, and (b) they derived tremendous benefit from being able to shape the services offered to them. This process had a twofold effect. First, there was the palpable benefit of obtaining what was needed (e.g., money for counseling, instruction in behavior management, an advocate present at an educational planning meeting, respite on Thursdays and Saturdays). The pilots confirmed that parents do know what is best for themselves and their children, that their requests are not ill-founded or frivolous, and that the fulfillment of these perceived needs greatly enhances their ability to care for their child at home. The second effect, though less palpable, had no less of a direct impact—being "master of your own destiny." Many of these families were accustomed to being told by professionals what they needed to do for their child. Having the tables reversed contributed tremendously to the families' own sense of self-respect, self-confidence, and confidence in their ability to care for their children.

Individualized Services

"Family driven" services necessarily entail individualization. The pilots demonstrated that individualized services will result in accomplishments that are as varied as the families themselves. Individualized cash assistance permitted one family to pay back rent so that they could apply for public housing and allowed another family to get a mechanized porch lift for their child. Individualized services meant that one family concentrated on finding an accessible summer camp for their child while another concentrated on advocating for increased educational supports. Although personalized and individualized services may be the right way to conduct all human service policy, the pilots demonstrated that it is especially important for families who have children with very unique disabilities. Each family served told a different story of how services were configured to meet their unique needs and how, therefore, the program enhanced in very concrete ways their daily efforts to care for their child. The pilots amply demonstrated that individualized support is highly dynamic and satisfying to the family.

Financial Assistance

All of the pilots incorporated a cash assistance component in some manner. Differences in administration largely depended on the decisions of the respective parent advisory councils. The pilots amply demonstrated the success of an individualized, flexibly administered, cash component. Typical concerns about cash assistance usually revolve around whether families can be trusted to use the cash in their own or in their child's own best interest. Requests for accountability mechanisms (such as vouchers, receipts, and payments made to vendors and not to families) arise in part from fears that families may frivolously or unwisely spend their additional income. Evidence from the pilots showed that in fact families can be quite meticulous about accounting for their cash, that they are more than willing to identify what they need to spend the cash on, and that the items purchased were completely within expectations of "right things" that the money should be spent on. For example, many low income families spent the cash on basic needs such as food, housing, clothing, and utilities. Other low and moderate income families used the cash to meet the extraordinary expenses encountered in raising their child with disabilities (e.g., counseling or testing for their child, out-of-pocket medical expenses, home modifications). Even the more "controversial" expenditures seemed to be sensible and worthwhile when viewed through the lens of family support and family empowerment (e.g., the one-time expenditure to help one family start a new in-home business, or the one-time expenditure that helped a family with the burial expenses of their deceased child who had a disability).

Conversely, the pilots demonstrated that when the cash component is not driven by families and not flexibly administered, the results can verge on absurdity. For example, in one pilot a worker persuaded families, sometimes against stated preferences, to buy clothes washers and dryers seemingly because large appliances represented an appropriate purchase. However, for one family, the washer and dryer wound up collecting dust because the family's electrical wiring could not support the appliances without disrupting the child's respiratory apparatus. Further, the pilot agency declined using cash assistance to enhance the wiring because the family had moved several times, and if they moved again the money would be "wasted."

Although the evidence from the pilots suggests that families can and should be trusted to make their own decisions about expenditures of cash assistance with few "strings attached," one exception to this finding emerged—cash assistance for families or individual parents who are known substance abusers. Clearly, this situation is the exception and not the rule, and therefore it makes no sense to structure a whole policy (such as not permitting cash to pass directly into the hands of the family) with negative ramifications on the many because of the infringements of a few. Nonetheless, the power of an addictive substance to influence the judgments of those in its grasp is well known and requires a forthright policy. Two pilot parent advisory councils wrestled with this difficulty, and perhaps its resolution should remain in the hands of those most directly associated with the governance of the program. One advisory council, for example, developed the policy that cash assistance could not be given to parents with known substance abuse unless they were actively getting help through a respected rehabilitation facility. Otherwise, the cash would go directly to another caretaker of the child (such as the grandmother), who would become a recipient of the family support services.

Parental Governance

All of the pilots incorporated a parent advisory council. The composition of the council and the degree to which it influenced pilot activities varied. However, the use of the council can only be regarded as a substantial success. Many parents who participated on the councils reported that their experiences resulted in tremendous personal growth. The opportunity to lend a voice that shapes events and that is respected and responded to by professionals had a lot of personal meaning, especially to parents unaccustomed to being taken seriously by social bodies outside of their personal sphere. Parents were challenged and rewarded by their opportunity to participate, and their influence made significant positive impact on the operation of the programs.

However, two cautions must be noted. One is that there was some evidence that parents, themselves unacquainted with parent empowerment principles, occasionally made rather conservative decisions that might be viewed as not being wholly in parents' interest. So, simply being a parent does not guarantee that a parent will reflect an empowering perspective. Parents, too, require training and technical assistance.

The second caution concerns how to take advantage of the momentum created by parent advisory councils. A feature shared by many of the councils in these pilots is that the parents, having gained tremendous personal resources from their participation, were then mobilized and motivated toward greater social action. Unfortunately, the time limited nature of the pilots did not permit continued avenues for social action. It became clear that future implementation of parent advisory councils should incorporate a mechanism for individuals to continue their growth as leaders and advocates for family support.

Administering Vehicles for Family Support

The pilots were administered by two very different supporting agencies. Both "mental health" pilots were conducted by parent associations. The two pilots in Philadelphia both utilized a more traditional social casework approach, and one was sponsored by a well-established child welfare agency. Some of the impressive successes of the mental health pilots can be attributed to the sponsoring agency. It makes sense that a family support program administered by an association of families with ties to the community would be best able to embrace the principles and practices of parent empowerment, and, therefore, associational bodies may be prime candidates for future programs. However, at least one of the pilots employing a more traditional social casework approach with trained social workers also amply demonstrated successful implementation of the same principles and practices. Therefore, there seems to be no need to discount more traditional approaches as providers of family support.

Time Limited Demonstration Programs

One problem emerged in all four pilots—the disruption of services to families due to the time limited nature of a demonstration program. Although the Pennsylvania Developmental Disabilities Council, in its request for proposals from bidders, asked potential grantees to specify how continuity of services would be assured after the grant lapsed, on the whole the pilots were not successful in providing continuity. In fact, some families were completely unaware that the pilot was ending. Others thought that a favorable independent evaluation would lead to continued funds. Still others, though aware of the time limited nature of the project, nonetheless experienced the termination of the pilot activities as a considerable personal loss. It was clear that time limited demonstration programs should be implemented only when care is taken to ensure a continuity of services after demonstration funding is ended.

RECOMMENDATIONS

The findings of the four pilots led to recommendations to the Pennsylvania Developmental Disabilities Council regarding the advancement of a family support agenda in the state. They defined underlying principles of a family support program and identified components of a successful service.

Family Support Principles

The first series of recommendations concerns the adoption of a set of principles, as follows:

Family Driven Services

"Family driven" is synonymous with the general notion of empowerment, that is, that families should be empowered to define *what* services they want delivered and *how* they want services to be delivered. It is opposed to the often prevailing (and paternalistic) notion that professionals "know what's best" for the family. It also implies a certain flexibility in the array of services offered, and the ability of families to choose among the services that are offered or available. In practice, the principle implies that the family is given the final authority in identifying what their needs are, in choosing service providers, and in designing a service plan.

Typical objections to family driven services arise from professionals who doubt that families know what is best. As the pilot evaluation indicates, many families do need assistance in identifying the range of supports that are available to them or in clarifying their options and wishes. However, the pilots also demonstrated that when this assistance is provided to families, they make positive choices that have palpable benefits. Often families may choose services that may not come have occurred to the professional but that turn out to be instrumental to their sense of ability to care for their child.

Family Focused Services

This principle stands in contrast to the child-centered focus that is the hallmark of more traditional services and implies that the whole family is the target of services. A typical objection to family-focused services is that public monies are best spent on the individual with disabilities in order to improve their quality of life and their opportunities for independence as adults. Family-focused services, however, proceed from the notion that the well-being of the child is inextricably linked to the well-being of the family. By taking care of the needs of the family, you are directly and fundamentally addressing the needs of the child. Moreover, it is presumed that assistance for the family in taking care of their child will ultimately result in less need for intervention from the public in other ways (e.g., out-of-home placement, or the public costs due to unemployment, divorce, or other possible negative consequence of raising a child with disabilities without assistance). The pilots demonstrated that family centered services are an efficacious way to help the child by helping the family.

Family Governed Services

This principle suggests that the design, review, and critical decisions related to service planning in family support should rest in the hands and authority of families themselves. This is another feature of family empowerment and implies that parents should assist in the design, implementation, and evaluation of family support programs.

Though parents should be in the majority on governing boards or councils, this principle does not preclude the participation of other relevant parties (i.e., professionals, administrators, and other community and civic representatives). Indeed, the pilots demonstrated that parent advisory councils themselves may need training or technical assistance in order to best carry out their responsibilities. However, the pilots also demonstrated that parent participation on advisory councils is tremendously enriching and empowering for the participants themselves, and it provides an important anchor by which services are moored to the needs and interests of families.

Parent-to-Parent Affiliation

A key finding of the four demonstration pilots was the importance and benefit of parent-to-parent affiliation. Whether through specific support groups, membership on advisory councils, or simply informal friendships, the linking of parents with each other emerged as a principal aid to families caring for a child with disabilities.

Individualized and Highly Flexible Supports

This principle affirms that the needs of families vary greatly and are unique to the circumstances of the individual families. It suggests that all service planning must be individualized, and that while there may be some cross family needs that warrant centralized planning (e.g., respite care), on the whole, the service plan will vary from family to family. The best family support will start with the families first rather than with designing a fixed set of service options.

Formation of an Active and Capable Constituency through Individual Supports and Group Efforts

Family empowerment as evidenced through the four pilots is a powerful force that transforms individuals and creates the energy and inspiration that can be tapped for wider advocacy and political activity. Service planning needs to recognize this outcome of family empowerment and capitalize on this energy.

Reliance on Community Resources

The principles of normalization and integration increasingly permeate all service planning for persons with disabilities. They assume that persons with disabilities have the human right to participate as full members of society. These principles argue against the creation of segregated services or environments that limit the interaction of persons with disabilities to paid staff and other people with disabilities. In terms of family support, this principle means that families should be able to use supports and services that are available to all members of the community rather than those that are characteristically used or designed for persons with disabilities.

Family Empowerment

All of the above principles are combined under this rubric. As a principle for service planning, the concept refers to practices that recognize and add to the family's mastery, capability, and knowledge of their own situation. Therefore, it is recommended that family empowerment continue to serve as the defining principle for service planning.

Components of a Successful Family Support Service

The second set of recommendations deals with the components of a successful family support service as listed and described below.

Noncategorical and Flexible Eligibility Criteria

The importance of a flexible noncategorical approach to eligibility determination was evidenced in the pilot evaluation. For example, an adolescent who used a wheelchair had been repeatedly turned down for services due to his exceedingly rare condition. However, the flexible eligibility criteria in the pilot permitted services and the installment of a porch lift, which greatly added to his and his mother's independence.

Parent Governing Councils to Be Employed at the Provider Level

The word "governing" is chosen over "advisory" because it is recommended that parents be given real authority and responsibility for program design and operations rather than functioning merely as an advisory body. The composition of the councils can be adjusted to include participation from nonparent members. However, it is recommended that the majority of persons be parents of children with a disability and be drawn, preferably, from the pool of actual service recipients.

The pilots demonstrated that family governing councils work successfully on the most immediate, local level. If family support is contracted out to provider organizations, it is recommended that the provider be required to employ a family governing council that is significantly composed of family members who are actually receiving services. To the extent that family support design and administration take place at another level (e.g., through the county), a governing council at that level is warranted.

Highly Skilled and Supportive Personnel

One of the other major findings of the family support pilot evaluation is the importance of staff who are knowledgeable about family supports in the community, who are capable of working with families to establish goals, and who have the ability to provide emotional support when necessary.

Parent Support Groups

This component is one manifestation of the principle of parent-to-parent affiliation. Though encumbered by logistical difficulties, on the whole the parent support groups (which often involved parent education) were one of the most valued aspects of the pilots. While continued exploration is needed regarding the use of professional leaders for the parent support groups or other features that may encourage participation, we recommend that any family support program should include this activity.

Financial Assistance

A major component of all four pilots was some form of cash assistance. Cash assistance is a natural outcome of the principles of family support.

If services are to be driven by the family and are to be responsive to individual needs, then cash is a critical component. For example, only cash assistance will help families pay for the parking and fuel costs to take their child to multiple medical appointments, only cash will pay high utility bills due to the respirator, and only cash will pay for the "extras" needed when a child returns home after a long hospitalization. For many of the low income families served by the pilots, the cash assistance went toward food, clothing, and utilities, allowing some relief to family budgets and the ability to "do more" for all members of the family.

While some form of cash assistance is clearly warranted, there is much variation across the nation in how cash assistance is delivered. Based on the findings of the pilot evaluations, the following recommendations in this regard are made:

- *No limitations should be placed on how the cash can be used or on what it can be spent.* Efforts to limit the scope of permissible purchases usually derive from two sources. One is a suspicion that families will abuse public monies for inappropriate purchases. The second is ambiguity over whether monies should rightfully go to family needs or should be child-focused. Supports for the family aid both the family and the child with a disability, and restrictions on purchases would be an unfortunate and unnecessary limitation. The evaluators consistently reported that purchases made by the families were within appropriate boundaries. Purchases typically followed the pattern reported in other cash subsidy programs (i.e., families with low income tend to use the cash assistance for provisional needs, and families of moderate means tend to use the cash for adaptive and recreational equipment related to the needs of the child with the disability).
- *No vouchers or other accountability mechanisms should be required.* Many schemes for cash assistance involve the use of vouchers, checks paid to service providers, requirements for receipts, or other documentation of purchases. All of these efforts revolve around the same distrust of families noted above. In keeping with the finding that families will not inappropriately use funds, requiring receipts or use of vouchers places an unnecessary bureaucratic burden on families, and tracking expenditures is a wasteful use of resources. While some tracking systems for family purchases may be useful for long-term evaluation purposes, efforts should be made to place as few reporting burdens on families as possible. Any other approach would be fundamentally disempowering.
- *Families should have the opportunity to explore purchasing possibilities with service coordinators.* Pilot evidence shows that families need an opportunity to discuss and obtain information on ways to use the subsidy. Many need both identification of the range of supports that their subsidy can buy and precise information and referral on how their subsidy can be used to the

fullest advantage (e.g., referral to charitable organizations that will pay for some or all of their expressed needs). An approach used in one pilot and in other family support programs is the use of a purchasing plan which, written in conjunction with the service provider, indicates what the family plans to use the subsidy for and what responsibilities the family and the service coordinator have to seek identified resources. Most families had no objection to the purchase plan, and many favored the opportunity to explore their options and set goals with a service coordinator.

- *The subsidy should consist of a standard amount geared to the severity of the child's disability; however, special discretionary funds at the local level should be available for families who are in unique or pressing circumstances, who are otherwise ineligible, or whose needs exceed the yearly allotment. An upper ceiling to family income should be implemented.* One pilot experimented with allocating cash assistance in differing amounts according to written "proposals" from parents regarding their needs. This proved to be a difficult process because advisory board members struggled with trying to assess the relative needs of one family compared to another. We propose that this process is too cumbersome, too resource consuming, and ultimately disempowering for families, who find themselves having to compete with each other for being the most deserving of funds. An equitable subsidy is recommended that is weighted toward children with the most severe disabilities on the assumption that the greater the disability, the greater the ancillary expenses and family stress experienced. However, we also recommend that a small budget be maintained for discretionary use at the local level for unusual needs that cannot otherwise be met by the subsidy.

Continued Opportunities for Parental Growth as Individuals and as a Constituency

A clear finding of the pilot evaluations is that family empowerment works, and when it does, it expands the potential for parents to become an active and capable voice in setting policy agenda, in driving policy efforts, and in creating increased local support. Any family support program must recognize and take advantage of the potential of this resource through ongoing guided efforts to channel parent energies into effective arenas.

Capacity to Address Unmet Service Needs

A final note on the inclusiveness of family support must be made. While the subsidy and service coordination will provide families with a range of supports not previously available, typical support services (e.g., specialized therapies and evaluations, respite care, transportation, early intervention, recreation programs) also need to be available. A cash subsidy will do no good for the family who requires a good behavioral therapist if no behavioral therapist is available. Therefore, an important feature of family support should be the ability to assess and rectify any service gaps in the local area.

CONCLUSION

Often, policy moves forward ignited by a passion to redress unmet needs and by a vision of new and better service principles and practices. Frequently, too, these movements come undone under the harsh light of unforeseen difficulties and unreachable hopes. The family support movement has obtained in some quarters uncritical acceptance that has not been tempered by the knowledge gained from "real life" implementation. The four Pennsylvania family support pilots, however, provided an opportunity to glimpse how family empowerment can be put into practice and what the main benefits and likely problems are of such an approach. The pilots gave direct support to the premise that family empowerment not only inspires, it also works.

Chapter 6 # Conclusions and Implications

Valerie J. Bradley

The preceding studies present a picture of emerging trends and themes in the provision of supports to families with children with mental retardation and other disabilities. Though this should not be considered an exhaustive nor a definitive review, the material does offer a series of suggestive analyses that highlight the content of a growing political movement as well as the outlines of an emerging system. The previous discussions also prompt some observations regarding the implications for evaluation, program design, and the necessary cautions that should be raised as family support moves from the realm of demonstration to becoming a mainstream element in the overall service system.

EVALUATION OF FAMILY SUPPORT

Many of the innovative family support programs around the country began as pilot or demonstration activities, such as those reviewed in chapters 4 and 5. While evaluations of such projects are key to a determination to extend such benefits statewide, some caveats should be applied. Pilots usually take place within a semi "hot house" environment in which high expectations are attached and much attention is paid to enterprise. As Weiss (1988) has noted, there is a danger in presuming that similar results will pertain when the program is expanded, especially if the subsequent supports are not adequately funded.

This in turn argues for ongoing evaluation of family support programs to ensure that the original intentions and goals of the programs are being respected and that resources continue to be adequate to meet the needs of the families and children who participate. Any innovation in human services has a tendency toward entropy or deterioration over time and thus needs to be rejuvenated periodically through systematic monitoring. An example of commitment to ongoing evaluation can be seen in the State of Michigan, where a professional evaluator has been assigned to review the results of that state's family support program since its inception (Herman, 1991).

In addition to evaluations that attempt to understand the impact of family support on the dynamics of the family, we need to develop relevant cost-benefit analyses (see also White, 1988; in Weiss & Jacobs). The analyses of services that have been conducted in the disability field over the past several years have tended to focus on the ability of an intervention to reduce institutionalization and therefore avoid the high cost of out-of-home placement. These types of analyses, however, are not as helpful in assessing the cost impact of family support for two reasons: Admission to institutions in many states is foreclosed, and the vast majority of families will keep their children at home regardless of the supports that they are offered.

Cost-benefit analyses of family support, therefore, should not necessarily focus on the more dramatic and explicit costs of institutionalization, but rather on the more subtle costs incurred by the family and in turn by the society because of the challenges of having a child with a disability. Such costs include the so-called "opportunity costs" associated with the care needs of a child with a disability including withdrawal from the work force and the postponement of training and promotional opportunities (see Agosta, chapter 4). These events ultimately diminish the family's earning capacity and ultimately its contribution to the state and federal tax base. Further, the stresses placed on the family, including those between mother and father, may result in divorce, poor educational achievement among siblings, and other indicators of dysfunction. These possible outcomes also have a social price.

Further, any evaluation of the impact of family support programs must be premised on a realistic assessment of the limitations of conducting such evaluations within a complex political, programmatic, and interpersonal context. As Jacobs and Weiss (1988) noted in their book on family support evaluation, "A flawless evaluation design according to the abstract canons of social science research may be of limited value; indeed evaluations often must trade off between neat scientific rigor and complex, but realistic, portrayal of programs" (p. 503). This suggests that the collection of data should be as parsimonious as possible and that all data elements should be central to ongoing policy assessment rather than of peripheral interest to the evaluator.

Because of the collaborative nature of the types of family support programs discussed in this monograph, evaluation should also represent a partnership among the evaluators, the families who are using the service, and those who provide family support. In this way, multiple perspectives will be reflected in determining the goals against which to measure the program and in designing the most useful, respectful, and expeditious means of soliciting information from families.

The degree of intrusiveness of the evaluation instruments is also an important issue—and one that can be addressed directly if families are involved in the evaluation design. Information gained during interviews conducted by staff at the Human Services Research Institute as part of evaluation around the country indicates that many family members resent being asked highly personal questions, such as frequency of sexual contact—especially if they do not understand the relevance of such questions to an understanding of family support. Maximizing the "family friendly" quality of the survey instrument is particularly important if it is the intention of the evaluator to collect information at multiple data points. In other words, families might be disposed to provide answers to questions they find distasteful during the first administration, but their willingness to be forthcoming will likely diminish over time.

In order to develop a body of information about the impact of family support programs nationwide, it will be important for those working in the field to find a common taxonomy to describe family support. Without this common understanding, it will be almost impossible to compare studies across sites. In some parts of the country, family support is equated with respite services and very little else. In other regions, family support encompasses a broad range of services, financial assistance, and case management. Thus, evaluators should be explicit about their definitions of family support and should work toward a common terminology and framework.

To date, many of the evaluations that have been conducted have focused on the positive benefits of family support to the person with a disability as well as to the family. However, for some families, supports have not always been successful in remediating stress and improving the family's quality of life. The next generation of research should provide more insight into those instances where family support fails and the factors—both within the family and within the service system—that may predict such failure.

Finally, evaluators of family support programs in the disability field must also take heed of what is transpiring in the family support movement taking root in the generic human services and child welfare field. An understanding of the similarities and differences in these currently separate movements will be important in understanding the ramifications of potential systems integration proposals (e.g., the creation of "Departments of Family Services") pending in some states.

PROGRAM DESIGN

The results of the evaluations and surveys highlighted in the monograph suggest some important lessons for those who are designing family support systems. Specifically, the role of the service coordinator or family facilitator emerges as central to the ability of the family to secure resources and to make connections in the community. As Agosta notes, families rated this facet of their family support program very highly. Among the many reasons why this is the case, not the least is the difficulty families face in gaining access to complex service systems. The role played by the family facilitator in these programs also differs from that of a conventional case manager because it involves more of a partnership or collaboration between the paid staff person and the family member. Finally, families report that just having a sympathetic person at the other end of the line who is willing to give advice, come over to help cope with a crisis, or simply listen is a significant support for them and their families.

The change in the role of case managers noted above raises an additional design issue—the importance of training and retraining to ensure that staff in family support programs have a firm grounding in the programmatic assumptions that underlie the program. Such training is crucial given the ways in which family support programs depart from more conventional services. For staff, this means developing more collaborative approaches and vesting more of the decision-making and determination of needs with the family. These approaches are not necessarily part of current training for case managers and other staff, and without an aggressive campaign to reorient existing personnel, standard operating procedures will pertain.

The evaluations reported in chapters 4 and 5 further suggest the importance of some form of flexible funding within family support programs in order to meet the idiosyncratic needs of families with children with disabilities. Given the extreme variability in the types of things that families say they need, it is virtually impossible to design a family support program that can anticipate all of these needs and provide for them. The only way to ensure that family support programs are capable of responding in a flexible fashion is by including a cash component. Although the family subsidy program in Michigan offers the most flexibility by providing families with "no strings attached," monthly stipends, there are many other ways of making cash available to families for specific purchases (e.g., through vouchers, cash reimbursement, etc.).

Knoll's report of interviews with families around the country graphically points out the difficulty that families face in attempting to gain access to services and the extent to which they are made to feel that they must "beg" for services or are demeaned for asking for help. This attitude not only disempowers families, it may dissuade some people from seeking needed services. The tendency to treat potential clients as supplicants rather than equals can be rectified by a strong affirmation of the principles of empowerment and family commitment as part of the design of any family support program. Such principles should not only be part of the specific mission of discrete family support agencies but should also be present in statute and regulation (see state family support laws in Colorado, New Hampshire, and Oregon, chapter 3).

A major way of ensuring that these principles are in fact reflected in program implementation is to create oversight mechanisms that involve families in a direct monitoring role. It follows that if family support programs are "family-focused," then families should be involved at various levels to ensure that programs continue to live up to the expectations that were initially vested in them. For instance, New Hampshire and Louisiana have included family supports councils as a key ingredient in their family support programs. These councils are vested with the responsibilities of evaluating the conduct of family support and, in the case of New Hampshire, of determining priorities and identifying providers. Including families in these capacities should provide an early warning system regarding any compromise on the original governing principles.

The needs of families are not only idiosyncratic, but span a number of agencies (e.g., health, social services, Social Security Administration, education, etc.). Services are currently organized in a way that puts the onus on the family to seek out and apply for services, resulting in an onerous burden for families who already face more than their share of time-consuming tasks associated with caregiving. In order to relieve families of some of this responsibility, designers of family support programs should build in an interagency component, whether through joint agency sponsorship, interagency councils, integrated agencies at the local level, or other ways.

One of the biggest challenges for those who design family support programs is to address the very real isolation and stigma faced by families with children with mental retardation and other disabilities. Such isolation can be seen in the strong need expressed by families to find recreational and leisure time activities for their families and in their anecdotal reports of shrinking social contacts resulting from the pressures of caregiving as well as the withdrawal of some friends and relatives from the family. Family support programs, therefore, should be designed to assist families to make connections in their communities and to take advantage of natural support systems in their own neighborhoods. Programs should also help families to identify integrated recreational programs and to ascertain the types of supports that might be required to successfully gain access to such community services.

LESSONS FOR THE FUTURE

The family support movement is being touted as a critical element in the emerging community system. Given this increased interest, it is important to explore some of the limitations of the programs as well as some realistic cautions. First, it is important to keep in mind that family support programs cannot substitute for the basic foundation supports, including health care, income assistance, parental leave opportunities, and day care. Family support programs should not, therefore, be sold to policymakers as the sole or sufficient intervention on behalf of families with children with disabilities but rather as "whatever it takes" over and above these basic safeguards to maintain a child in the home.

We must also recognize that even the best family support programs will not, in every case, prevent the placement of a child out of the home—either temporarily or permanently. Not all families will be able to meet the challenges of a family member with a disability, and some families will seek placement in order to preserve the integrity and functioning of the remainder of the family. In these instances, public policy must assure that other resources are available and that such alternatives are also family-based (e.g., adoptive families, specialized foster families, etc.). Family support policy that stresses the maintenance of children within natural families should not be used as a sword to diminish or attack those families who choose to make a placement.

Further, there is a danger that family support programs will be sold as a way of reducing the demand for services and reducing waiting lists. Family support should not be seen as a substitute for providing services to adults who, like their brothers and sisters, deserve the opportunity to pursue their lives as independent adults. If family support becomes a thinly disguised means of shifting the responsibility for people with disabilities back onto the family, the basic principles underlying the movement will be betrayed, and the trust of families in the service system will be further eroded.

In line with this issue is the need to address how adult children will be treated within family support programs. Clearly, many adults—both those with disabilities and those without—continue to live with their parents after they reach the age of majority. Recent economic contractions coupled with inflated housing prices have made this phenomenon more prevalent in the past decade. Thus, it would seem arbitrary to design eligibility requirements that cut-off entry to those families with a family member over 21 years. However, we should also be sensitive to the emerging adult and the importance of ensuring that his or her choices regarding where to live are respected. In other words, family support for families with adult family members should be provided when it is determined with certainty that the wishes of the person with a disability as well as the family are taken into account.

As family support gains legitimacy in disability policy, it will also be important to ensure that it is not simply a white, middle class program. This fear is supported by the fact that the political movement for family support has been led primarily by middle class and upper middle class families. If family support programs are also to reflect the needs of minority families and families living in poverty, policymakers and program administrators will have to include these constituencies in program design and will have to assess the most efficacious ways of reaching out to these communities.

The need for family support should also be seen as an important issue for women, who are the primary caregivers for children with disabilities in the overwhelming number of cases. Many women have had to put their lives on hold (e.g., professionally, educationally, etc.) to take on the responsibility of caring for their child. It is also often incumbent on women in the home to make the necessary connections with the community, to develop supports in the neighborhood, and to negotiate the maze of services including the educational system. The implications of this frequent division of labor suggest that the push for family support should be linked to other women's issues, such as parental leave, child support, and day care. Additionally, those who espouse the values of family support should be cautioned not to overly romanticize the role of mother as caregiver in order to free her to pursue those personal goals that many other women are now able to pursue.

Finally, in keeping with a concern about perpetuation of dependence, policy and program planners should consider incorporating ways for families to make contributions back to the program and to other families. Many families are uncomfortable with the one-way character of publicly subsidized supports and report positive feelings about programs that offer them the opportunity to give back something. This can be accomplished in a variety of ways, including bartering arrangements in which families can contribute their talents to others in the community, self-help groups where families can share their experiences and expertise, and the use of families as service brokers, coordinators, and advocates for other families.

CONCLUSION

This monograph is an initial effort to flesh out the outlines of an emerging service paradigm. Since the program is still somewhat formative, the analyses and findings should be treated in a similar fashion. One thing does appear certain, however. The family support movement has gained substantial momentum and acceptance, and its premises are attractive to those who espouse a leaner, more consumer-focused, and locally-based human services system. The challenge is to ensure that the excitement and innovation that accompany these initial efforts can be sustained in the face of budget constrictions and the tendency in human services toward inertia and routinization.

REFERENCES

Herman, S. (1991). Use and impact of a cash subsidy program. *Mental Retardation, 29*, 253–258.

Jacobs, F. H., & Weiss, H. B. (1988). *Evaluating family programs.* New York: Modern Application of Social Work.

Weiss, H. B. (1988). Family support and education programs: Working through ecological theories of human development. In H. B. Weiss & F. H. Jacobs (Eds.), *Evaluating family programs.* New York: Modern Application of Social Work.

White, K. (1988). Cost analyses in family support programs. In H. B. Weiss & F. H. Jacobs (Eds.), *Evaluating family programs.* New York: Modern Application of Social Work.

About HSRI and the Editors

The Human Services Research Institute

Since the Human Services Research Institute (HSRI) began operation in 1976, it has participated in a range of disability-related policy and research studies for federal and state governments. Over the past several years, HSRI staff have conducted evaluations, provided consultation and technical assistance, and facilitated policy reforms in 30 states and the District of Columbia and have conducted studies for major federal agencies including the Department of Housing and Urban Development, the National Institute of Mental Health, the National Institute of Disability and Rehabilitation Research, the Administration of Developmental Disabilities, and the Assistant Secretary of Planning and Evaluation of the Department of Health and Human Services.

The professional staff at HSRI come from a variety of backgrounds to form a comprehensive base of expertise that includes psychology, social work, political science, sociology, special education, health administration, and business administration.

HSRI's aim is to provide information and analysis to policy makers concerned about improving and expanding opportunities for persons with disabilities and their families by developing supports and services that will enhance their abilities to participate fully as equals in their communities.

Valerie J. Bradley

Valerie J. Bradley has been President of HSRI since its inception in 1976, and in that capacity has developed and managed a wide range of projects in mental health, developmental disabilities, substance abuse, and other human service programs, and has provided consultation to over 40 organizations.

Recent projects include research on financial supports for home care (National Institute on Disability and Rehabilitation Research), assessment of decentralization in Scandinavia, development of national standards for developmental disabilities councils as well as protection and advocacy services, technical assistance to ten states in developing broad-based family support programs, and the development of a national clearinghouse on family support services.

Bradley holds a master's degree in political science from Rutgers. Among her publications are *Quality Assurance for Individuals with Developmental Disabilities: It's Everybody's Business* with Henry Bersani, *The Dynamics of Change in Residential Services for Persons with Developmental Disabilities* with Mary Ann Allard, and *Deinstitutionalization of Developmentally Disabled Persons: A Conceptual Analysis and Guide*.

James A. Knoll, Ph.D.

James Knoll is currently Associate Director of the Developmental Disabilities Institute at Wayne State University, Detroit, Michigan, where he continues his interest in family support programs and supported living for adults with disabilities. During 1988-90 he was Senior Research Analyst at HSRI, where he directed a variety of research, including evaluation of family support projects in Pennsylvania and Illinois, an assessment of the current status of family supports in the United States, and evaluation of specialized case management services to families providing home care to chronically ill children (Maternal and Child Health Program).

Knoll earned his doctorate in mental retardation at Syracuse University and his master's in special education at Hunter College. Recent publications are *Community Integration for People with Severe Disabilities* (co-editor) and *The Nonrestrictive Environment: On the Community Integration of People with the Most Severe Disabilities* (co-author).

John M. Agosta, Ph.D.

John Agosta is Senior Research Associate at the HSRI office in Salem, Oregon, where he provides policy analysis, develops data collection strategies, designs and conducts statistical analyses, and reports project results. One ongoing project is a comparative, indepth analysis of the decentralization of human services in Denmark, Sweden, and Norway relative to systems in the United States. Another aims to identify, generate, and disseminate materials to help family support advocates translate theory into practice, including quality criteria, exemplary programs, and strategies for self-advocacy and funding. He is also analyzing conditions affecting job coaches, their changing roles, status, and management, and he is examining options for system reform in regional service structures in various states including Idaho and Hawaii.

With a background in psychology and special education, Agosta earned his doctorate in special education and rehabilitation at the University of Oregon. He has published and presented with many professional and disability organizations.